With You Always

Stories of a Heaven Bound Alaskan

Paul A. Weimer

With You Always
by Paul A. Weimer

Printed in the United States of America

Library of Congress Control Number: 2002100982
ISBN 1-931232-97-0

Xulon Press
11350 Random Hills Road
Suite 800
Fairfax, VA 22030
(703) 279-6511
XulonPress.com

With You Always

Walking onward, going upward, closer every day,
Soon we'll be there; soon we'll see
where all our treasures lay!
Watching for Him, looking to Him,
living in God's plan:
He will come then, we shall rest
when Jesus comes again!

Paul Weimer

Contents

Preface ix

Acknowledgements..xi

Chapter One
Early Road...1

Chapter Two
Builders 5

Chapter Three
Friends and the Friend 11

Chapter Four
Homesteader Years...17

Chapter Five
It's a Flying North...25

Chapter Six
Soldotna...33

Chapter Seven
Hunting and Fishing for Men...................................41

Chapter Eight
Drivers of Cars and Airplanes...................................51

Chapter Nine
Earthquake...57

Chapter Ten
Tests...61

Chapter Eleven
The Spirit of God and Other Spirits............................67

Chapter Twelve
Flying Is … 73

Chapter Thirteen
The Long Night...79

Chapter Fourteen
Discriminating...89

Chapter Fifteen
Quick! Do Something 95

Chapter Sixteen
Remote 99

Chapter Seventeen
Both Here and Coming 107

Poem
The Lord is There (Ezekiel 48:35)...........................113

Footnotes 115

Preface

══════════════

I was still a boy when I first came across Proverbs 3:5-6, believed it, and determined to make it mine. "Trust in the Lord with all thine heart, and lean not unto thine own understanding. In all thy ways acknowledge Him, and He shall direct thy paths." From childhood I have known the veracity of God's word and the complete believability of its promises. Experience has proven the trust and solidified the truths in personal knowledge. Early on I took Solomon's advice as a motto, "Fear God and keep His commandments; for this is the whole duty of man."

Encouraged by many to put down on paper certain events in a rather simple life, I submit these, that I might in some small way glorify Him who is my rock, my fortress, and my deliverer; My God, my strength, in whom I will trust; and my shield, and the horn of my salvation, and my high tower. (Psalm 18:2)

Since He, in sovereign power, "works all things together for good to them that love God, to them who are the called according to His purpose," we can expect to know Him better, and to be better through the events of life if we have hidden His word in the heart and continue to do so.

Also, individuals often have a profound and positive effect on another's life, while they may not even be aware of it. There have been many like that for me. Many helpers have been sent my way; friends for whom I thank my God who gave them.

Acknowledgements

Many thanks to Christina Weimer, Rebecca Hibpshman, and Danielle Page for their welcomed suggestions and their sacrificial and valuable help in typing, correcting, and preparing this for the publisher.

—*Paul A. Weimer*

Where I attended first grade in Pennsylvania.

On way to Alaska – clean up stop

CHAPTER ONE

The Early Road

I n those days a lot of people in the hills of Western Pennsylvania pictured Alaska as a land of perpetual ice and snow, where everybody in the frozen tundra lived in igloos. Even worse, my dad and uncles had very little interest in things spiritual. They considered preachers to be "off the wall," and second class citizens—probably a bit warped. So, of all places and things, to go to Alaska with the view to preach the gospel was industrial strength foolishness.

On the day that Esther and I left with our eighteen month old, Becky, a young well meaning life insurance agent appeared at the old house, determined to sell us, or saddle us, with a policy to cover us for this exceedingly dangerous adventure.

"I'm very concerned," said he, "about you starting on this trip without adequate insurance."

Looking back I wonder if he was more concerned with the security of his own pocket book! I also wonder if the Apostle Paul had enough insurance for his really perilous journeys. Or did Jonah? Now, some years later, I know we had the very best insurance.

> "Through many dangers, toils and snares I have
>   already come—
> 'Tis grace hath brought me safe thus far—and
>   grace will lead me home."[1]

Our trip north was unforgettable. There are places and circumstances we encounter that beggar description and can only be appreciated first hand. A hundred travelogues on places like Israel or Egypt will never teach you about them like walking their streets. The 1500 miles of gravel road between Seattle and Anchorage in those days was an experience for the hardy. Mechanical breakdowns, broken windows, broken headlights, and blown out tires were common and to be expected by all who traveled there. Drivers carried spare electrical parts, or whatever other parts, that may be needed to repair breakdowns. A bar of laundry soap, Fels Naptha, was handy to rub into gas tank holes made by flying rocks.

The Frazer River Canyon was terrific. With super steep grades and cliffhanger wooden bridges, bringing out repeated cries, "Go slow! Go slow!" from my wife, Esther. Somewhat later we would return to British Columbia to help missionary friends who were establishing a church there. The worst part of the trip, taking a toll on the equipment, was from Quesnel, BC, to Dawson Creek. That section was rough, rocky, crooked, and muddy.

People used to say that Alaska is the only place in the world where one could stand knee deep in mud with the dust blowing in your face and freeze to death all at the same time. One January trip with the temperature at minus 40 degrees Fahrenheit, our rig just quit! In about thirty minutes a brand new truck with a cozy warm cab stopped. The driver was enroute to Alaska. Perfect timing! I found our problem with the coil and was able to repair it in warmth!

Later that week we crossed the Yukon border in to Alaska. It was 65 below. You have to feel it to enjoy it. We did not travel at night under those conditions, but looked for motels with heated garages. At times, temperatures inside the garage may be 15-20 degrees below zero, but at least the engine would turn over.

Summer travel was, of course, better if you could tolerate the dust. Some small streams had no bridge, but the road went through anyway. We met a fast moving truck on a curve and there was no way to escape the gravel he threw, wiping out our side window.

The road of life—wherever it goes is going to be filled with surprises, unexpected things, wonderful things, and sometimes losses. Perhaps a desperate financial need, a medical atomic bomb, or the sudden reversal of trusted friends. They all go into the book of memories along with the beautiful things and the faithfulness of the Good Shepherd. In the end you arrive full at the desired haven singing, "The Lord is good, tell it wherever you go."

Under a clear blue sky, we topped the hill and started down the road into Homer. The waters of Kachemak Bay rimmed by mountains and glaciers made it a setting of grand beauty. The famous Homer Spit, running four miles out into the bay, and the blanket of fireweed blossoms covering the hillside and roadside was spectacular, transforming the dust of a gravel road into rose petals.

En route to Alaska

Spooling in the net.

CHAPTER TWO

Builders

Dale and Bea Davis had planted a church in Homer three years previously. The population there numbered about one-thousand people. Some having come from as far away as Washington, DC. Both church and missionary made home in what was called the Old Husky Building. Built of three-sided logs, it had previously housed a garage and a pool hall.

This part of Alaska took some getting used to. The water was not drinkable in the house and if left to stand awhile, worms would mysteriously appear. There was no indoor plumbing in the Old Husky Building, and the nearest outhouse was 70 feet away at the end of a slippery plank. Moose were a common sight there, too, often running down the busy gravel roads.

Many residents used Ford tractors, with a small box mounted behind the seat for transportation around town. Equipped with half-tracks, they were great rigs for harvesting coal off the beach and for the twenty to twenty-five mile runs to hunting areas back in the hills.

Local store prices were very high; many residents would order a year's supply of groceries to be delivered via ship from the "Lower 48," referred to in those days as the "Outside." (I guess that meant we were insiders.)

A name made common back then was "Sourdough"—which meant you were sour on Alaska but lacked the dough to leave.

The nearest hospital then was in Seward, 150 miles up the road. The other option one could consider was a thirty-minute float plane ride across the Bay to the village of Seldovia, where the Seventh Day Adventists operated a small four-room hospital. A man by the name of Dr. Provantia flew back and forth from Seldovia to Homer several times a week for those who needed medical care. Esther flew with him to Seldovia for the birth of our son, Dan. Two years later it was Hope that was to be born, and Esther made the trip again. This time she flew in another small floatplane. I don't think she ever did get comfortable in any flying contraption.

The fledgling Grace Baptist Church of Homer (now Glacier View Baptist) had purchased property for a church, under direction of Dale Davis. The acreage had two houses, one of which was to be used to house the missionary family while the other would be extensively remodeled to house the new church. All the interior partitions would be moved and the entire building would be turned to face the road.

However, priority one was the outhouse. Since neither building had an inside bathroom, the outside bathroom was pretty important. The problem was, it had been way overused and filled beyond capacity. I'll let your imagination fill in the gruesome detail. How was I to solve such a monumental task of removal and cleaning?

No engineer came to offer help. No one else did either. The thing was located underneath a grove of large spruce trees standing between the two houses. My first thought, with a smile, was to burn it. Then I reconsidered, "What if the trees catch fire, and then the houses?" That would have given both the church and me some kind of sudden popularity.

Slowly, out of deep meditations, a plan began to develop. I would dig a very deep hole out behind the house, and over it I would construct a brand new outhouse. No government agencies or environmentalists would interfere, for there were none back then. That part of the project was soon complete (a two-holer) except, it still needed a door.

Some teenage boys stopped by one day, looked at my house, and mentioned that we could get by without a door by simply posting a sign that directed any users to close their eyes while inside. I decided to build a door.

I became skilled at outhouse construction, learning as I went along. I built a fine outhouse in a different town later. That same night it rained long and hard, soaking the ground so much that the whole thing was swallowed up into its own hole. Thankfully, no one was inside.

Phase two of the Homer project was the removal of that old outhouse. I would wait for a good southeast wind to blow and set the thing on fire, and pray that the overseeing Lord would prevent the trees from catching fire. So the wind blew, the trees weren't even scorched, and a terrible mess was burned—purged with fire. The outhouse, once the coldest place in Alaska, ended its service via blazes.

The next job was the prospective church house. At twenty-four years of age, I was not a very accomplished builder; although by now, I had already built a doghouse and an outhouse. The best advice I received was to go down to the beach, locate some large drift logs, approximately forty feet long, and bring them to the site. Next, I was to find some house jacks with which to raise the building and place the logs under it (to act as rollers). Then, I was to set the building upon the logs, roll the building to the desired site, jack it up again, remove the rollers, set permanent logs, and let the house down in place on its new log foundation. Simple! Unfortunately, no one said that the ground there was soft and that a house jack would bury itself before even lifting the building an inch. Great!

My friend, Frank Wise, who had trusted Christ, knew how to have sympathy and could usually tell who needed it. He could tell that I needed it, so he loaned me his jeep.

Getting the logs to the site was the best part of the job. I had worked as a log skidder back in Pennsylvania so I had considerable experience with moving logs. With Frank's jeep, I skidded those 40-foot-long logs off the beach right up through the middle of town to our church site.

Then the real work began. After weeks of digging and grunting, mud, and pushing, we finally got it to the desired position. We rebuilt the interior of the building and had a rather crude but comfortable unit that would accommodate 50-60 people for church services.

It was while I was working under that building, and all covered with mud, that a well known homesteader (who later became a state senator) stopped by. Hollering at me he insisted, "Come out from under there and talk!" I had heard that he was an atheist and, being already impatient with the interruption, I kept on working.

I have never been able to figure out why an intelligent man cannot recognize the ample evidence of beauty and design, and know that organization and design require intellect. Or why he would rather dream that he came from a monkey than conclude that he came from the Word of God. He persisted until I crawled out and invited him over to the house. We discussed "religion" at great length, and I tried to present the gospel of salvation in Christ as clearly as possible. I do not know whether he ever surrendered to the truth, but heard later that some of his children had.

Regarding Evolution, a humorous joke reads as follows:

"Mama," said the little girl. "Is it true that we came from monkeys?"

Mama replied, "I don't know. I didn't know your father's people very well."

It is obvious that there are two distinct and different types of people in our world. More than once, I have had people from both classes point this out. There are those who are in the family of God, who have believed in the Savior, Jesus Christ, and have experienced the new birth. They have been regenerated by the Holy Spirit who works through the eternal Word of God (1 Peter 1:21). Then there are others who are outside of the family of God. These reject Christ or ignore Him and therefore, are not "Born of God" as stated in John 1:12-13. They live and walk according to the course of this world (Ephesians 2:2-3). Their only hope lies within their own accomplishments or human works—though proven a failure. They are without hope. Their moral standards are of their own making and therefore as variable as their appetites and desires.

Without God we are without hope. To all such people, the invitation is, "Come," and by faith, enter into God's family. It would seem that nothing in these short lives could match the importance of getting out of this life alive. In all history there has been only One who came out of the grave to live an endless life. Why gamble with life? "What will a man give in exchange for his soul?" Why trade away eternity for a day? Why speculate about the changing philosophies of dying men? Why not trust the one who lives forever? All the other religious leaders are dead! Why follow a loser!

Cutting wood for stoves

Remote river bar

CHAPTER 3

Friends and the Friend

Bill Kvasnikof was a real friend. He was admired for his various skills from carpentry to playing the accordion. He ran a trap-line each winter with a dog team and commercial fished during the summers.

In all his wilderness travels, he carried a rusty Winchester 22 rifle, with which he had killed moose, black bear, and even a large Kodiak brown bear. As he related that story, he had wondered whether the 22 could dispatch a brown bear.

One day, as he was cruising a bay on Kodiak Island in his 40-foot fishing boat, he spotted a likely bear out on the grass tidal flats. He ran his skiff onto the beach, got out and worked his way to a small knoll fairly close to "Mr. Bear." Aiming carefully, he squeezed the trigger and placed a little bullet in the great bear's lungs. This caused the bear to simply slap at the miniscule wound as he continued feeding in the grass. Again Bill shot at the same spot, and again the bear reacted with a slap. I have forgotten how many times Bill followed that procedure as the bear continued eating the grass, then finally dropped dead!

I was standing beside Bill once on another beach and saw him kill three geese with a single shot. Pretty good! That day I shot a seal from his rocking boat, which was legal to do back then. I then brought it onboard and skinned it. I noticed him watching from the bridge, and was happy afterward to hear him say, "You cleaned that up so well. You can skin a seal anytime on my boat!"

At that time, Bill and his family lived in the village of Ninilchik where there was no high school. Bill asked if his son, Erling, could stay with us that year so he could attend the local secondary school. We were happy to have him. He attended our youth meetings, listening often to the Gospel, but as far as I know never surrendered to Christ.

Many years later I was with Bill and Erling on a very dark and stormy night, trying to make Kodiak Harbor. The 40-foot seiner was tossed with waves crashing over the pilot-house. Visibility was almost nothing. Erling was at the wheel. I was standing beside him when he picked up a light—way off in the darkness. He took a heading for it. After awhile, another light appeared. These men, accustomed to such severe conditions, trusted the lights and followed them through the storm until we reached safe harbor.

I had asked Erling, as he piloted through the storm, why he had never trusted Christ as his Savior. He responded, "I guess I saw too many inconsistencies."

I had hoped he would stop looking at people, for they often fail to shine the true light. However, there is a light that never fails and always leads us home. Jesus said, "He that followeth me shall not walk in darkness, but shall have the light of life." And how vital it is for the Christian to walk and talk a lifestyle reflecting that true light. Someone is watching, some other sailor, you may not know who, till you get to Heaven.

"If you have named the name of Jesus, if you're

known as one of His,
Remember that the world is watching to see how
   your victory is.
They'll accept what they see and know you to be,
They'll judge by your life alone."[1]

One winter Bill asked me to help him pack beaver traps to a series of lakes he thought would be productive. We strapped on our snowshoes, loaded the traps on our pack boards, and headed for the nearest lake, six miles off the road. The country was rather flat and we made a straight line, arriving at the desired spot. He did not use a compass, nor were there any outstanding landmarks such as streams or mountains to guide us, yet we never got off course or lost our heading. However, the trip turned out to be a disappointment, because upon arriving at the first beaver house, we noticed airplane ski tracks. It was a sure sign that someone else had arrived ahead of us and claimed our fur-bearing critters.

One of the wonderful treasures of the Christian life is that of knowing the great and unfailing Shepherd Guide. His word says that He will never leave us ever! (Hebrew 13:5) He is never confused, never surprised, never loses His way, never short of provisions, or strength. Also, He transmits his strength to the believer who trusts in Him (Isaiah 40:28-29). That is something no other Guide can do, not even the doctor.

There is no searching of His understanding. He can show us the best way—the way of His will. "Your ears will hear a voice behind you saying, 'This is the way, walk ye in it.'" It is a rich possession indeed to know that He is personally interested and active for us, assuring us a successful and safe arrival at the goal. Wherever I have gone, I find He has already been there.

Often I have looked over stretches of natural beauty defying description: a clump of bright blue or yellow flowers in the middle of a rock covered mountainside: a magnificent golden eagle in its nest atop a great, granite spire: the white sheep surviving in a harsh and hostile climate, way north of the Arctic Circle, feeding in a pasture in a high mountain valley: mountainous waves cresting on the shore of a sea in rage, yet held in bounds.

I've looked and wondered how a man could fail to see the hand of God. Then I remember that, because of sin, men and women are by nature rebels against God, and, as we are taught in Romans, chapter 5, His enemies until conquered by the immeasurable love of God in Christ. "The invisible things of Him from the creation of the world are clearly seen, being understood by the things that are made, even His eternal power and Godhead..." (Romans 1:20). Peter adds,"...they are willingly ignorant..." (2 Peter 3:5), and willingly because, at enmity with God.

Once a person submits to reason, recognizing that any orderly effect must have a corresponding cause, that moment you say, "God is," you also say by nature of the case that you are responsible to Him.

> When you walk along the rooftops of God's
>   mountains in the sky,
> Where you can see forever and beyond.
> Beholding breathtaking wonders still unspoiled
>   by human hands,
> Then everywhere you look you see His face.
>
> By that wee babe's little cradle you have seen
>   that look of love,
> When that gift of life's love came from the Lord.
> Whether sunsets, diamonds, roses or in nature's
>   heaving power,
> Just everywhere you look you see His face.

As you look within the pages of God's wondrous
Book of love,
And read how Jesus came from Heaven above,
How he died to win your pardon, gave His life
    that you might live—
In Christ you see the image of God's face.

Oh, there is none other like Him! There is none
    so wondrous fair,
Truth and goodness, love and power, He is
    always there.
In my need His grace and goodness more than
    fills my hearts desire,
And everywhere I look, I see His face.

We are not just animals. Animals walk on four feet, looking down for satisfaction. God made man upright to look up for satisfaction.

I commercial fished on the Clam Gulch beach with a man who was a close friend of mine. His name was Frank Rusk. He was an intelligent man who held a degree from Texas A&M. He and his family had moved up from Texas, bought a sawmill, and built a beautiful log home. He related to me how he had been an atheist, often arguing with others over his humanistic philosophies, and ridiculing those who believed in the Bible. However, he started noticing the order of nature, the regular changing of the seasons, the rising and falling of the tides, the annual return of the salmon, the orderly hydrology of cloud to water to earth to river to ocean and back to cloud again. He saw a thousand "infallible proofs" of the great creator-maintainer God, and was convinced. His struggle to deny self and surrender to God was a long battle, but finally he said yes and received Christ. The light then came on, and he became a shining Christian.

Beginning Sterling Baptist church

Completed church and parsonage in Sterling

CHAPTER 4

Homesteader Years

It was mid-winter when we arrived in Sterling to take over the work there, and a cold winter it was, with the temperature dropping to 50 degrees below zero that year. Several times during the month of March, there had been a temperature change of 80 degrees in only twenty-four hours. During the night, the temperature would dip to -40 degrees, and then peak to a blistering 40 degrees above zero the next day.

Electricity had not yet arrived then. Like most of our neighbors, we carried water from a beautiful spring that never froze over.

The Barkley family had moved to the location a couple of years earlier and secured good property from the government on which to build a church, and roughed in a house with blankets for partitions, in which they started a Sunday school. They were hard workers! They stayed on until summer while Milt and I framed up a 24' X 32' church house. Mr. Barkley had taken a job in a sawmill, taking his wages in lumber with which to build. That summer, they left Alaska for Ohio where he pastored for many years.

I hauled shavings from the mill with which to insulate the

church-house walls. We used a two-barrel wood stove to heat it. (The bottom 50-gallon drum was the firebox, while the top drum was fashioned so that the hot smoke circulated through it before exiting the smokestack.)

Meanwhile, it was another cold winter. Often times in the morning, the water bucket in the kitchen would be found frozen over.

The house we lived in had two barrel stoves—one up stairs and one in the basement. It was a full-time job to cut wood, feed the three stoves, carry fresh water from the spring, and carry used water out! The basement wall on which our house rested began to self-destruct. The wall heaved and buckled, the cement floor heaved wonderfully. If left alone, the house would have soon eaten itself.

Kermit Dowse helped me cut and bring to the site several large logs. We moved the house to the side, filled the basement hole with gravel, and sat the house down on a foundation of large spruce logs. Perfect and solid!

About ninety people lived in the entire area called Sterling, covering an area roughly thirteen miles long by two miles wide. After awhile we got to know the local dogs by name.

We would drive all the main roads and homestead trails to pick up adults and kids for our services. Esther learned to play the little pump organ, even mastering the first half of the wedding march. That's all she needed to get the bride down the aisle.

It was an education to keep the only vehicle, a Chevy carry-all, running. It would not start if the temperature dropped below -20 degrees. There were no engine block heaters, and no electricity anyhow. So we would set the alarm clock to ring at two-hour intervals throughout a cold night to waken us to go out, start the car and let it warm up. If that didn't work, you pumped up the Coleman blazo stove and slid it under the oil pan. Then you covered the hood with blankets or tarps to hold the heat. That will surely bring back some fond memories for the old timers.

My friend had a short fuse (and sometimes the finesse of a D-8 cat). His family's gasoline-powered washing machine was a temperamental critter that exasperated him to a spasm of anger. He threw the thing in his truck and carried it to the dump. After cooling down, his wife made him go back and retrieve it.

A homesteader once got so vexed with his vehicle, that he grabbed a hammer and punched out the headlights!

Alaska then was a harsh and rugged place, demanding a lot and requiring tough people to settle it. Most people around us were homesteaders. The law provided that you could file a claim on land up to 160 acres. Then, before title was granted, you had to clear a percentage of it, cut and remove the trees and stumps, plow, cultivate, raise a crop, and build a habitable dwelling. All must pass inspection by the officials. It was long, hard work.

Moreover, few of those dear folks were well financed, so they had to work for wages, which meant a lot of traveling in either the commercial fishing industry, to military bases, in construction and up on the oil fields, requiring them to be absent for extended periods. We spent many hours and days helping some to "prove up" their homesteads by cutting down trees, removing stumps, feeding and butchering pigs, cows, chickens, etc. We hunted with them, fished with them, ministered to them, and saw some of them surrender to Christ.

Bill Gilligan was a bachelor living up the road in his cabin. He had a bad reputation, including a history of time spent in prison. On a cold November day he came and asked me to help him pack out a moose he had killed a half-mile off the road. When we arrived at the carcass it was well frozen. It was quite a job, but when we finally got it out to the road and to his cabin, he generously gave me a large choice chunk of loin. However, the piece of meat turned out so tough it was impossible to eat. I don't know how long the dog gnawed on it.

Bill never trusted the Lord, and a few years later during a drunken party in his cabin, he killed a woman with his ax.

I was invited to go on a hunt along the Kenai River with two other men. In those days the other side of the river was not yet developed and not a soul lived there, making it a good area for moose. After a while, we beached the boat. We separated and proceeded to hunt. Perhaps an hour had gone by when I heard one of those men fire off a gunshot. I then returned to the boat, expecting to help pack meat. It seemed like ages before they appeared. When they finally showed up, I noticed their rather sheepish faces.

I said, "What was shot?"

"Oh, just a goose," Jimmy said.

A week or so went by, and one of them gave me a nice tasty chunk of meat. I added two plus two. They had shot an illegal cow on our hunt, but didn't want to get the preacher in trouble, so, they kept their secret. We enjoyed the meat, asking no questions for conscience sake.

Again I was visiting a friend in his wilderness cabin, many miles from town. We got around to discussing moose. I remarked that this was the first year in many that I had not had success hunting. He asked, "Didn't you get a moose?" I simply said, "No." He then disappeared out the back door. In minutes he returned with a nice, fresh piece of loin. I asked no questions, just got in the airplane and flew home.

A fish and game officer approached me once with the request that I report to him any illegal game kills among the homesteaders that I knew. But, I could not do that. We always tried to be scrupulously careful about game laws for our testimony sake, but I knew that those people lived on the edge of need and that nothing was wasted. We knew what hunger was when the meager dollars ran out, leaving nothing to eat for days but macaroni, without the cheese! We were thankful for macaroni and we sympathized with those guys.

Lee and Bev Vansycle stopped by one cold winter night. We always enjoyed their good fellowship and had a pleasant evening. About 11:00 P.M. that night, we followed them out to the car to say good bye. Standing there in the sub-zero darkness we heard a faint and far away cry for help. We could barely hear it, but then it came again, unmistakably. We got in the car and drove toward the river a mile and a half away. But there we heard nothing. Back at the house, it came again. "H-e-l-l-l-l-p!" We then hurried to another place up the river to the Sterling Post Office.

A hunter across the Kenai River had lost his way, wandered for hours, and stumbled out on the riverbank and saw the lights of the post office and grocery store on the other side. By that time he was desperate with cold and one's mind does not work well under such circumstances. He stood there crying out for help, and when no one responded, he decided to wade across the ice filled river. A few steps into the rapid, frigid waters and he was over his head. Frantic, he thrashed around until his hand caught an overhanging tree branch and he was able to pull himself back to shore. Completely soaked in the sub-zero cold, he was now worse off than before. Walt Peterson, from the store, heard his cry finally, put a boat in the river, crossed over and rescued him. We arrived as Walt was pushing and coaxing him up the bank.

Once again this rugged unforgiving country provided a vivid illustration of vital spiritual truth. "It is not in man that walketh to direct his steps" (Jeremiah 10:23). We hunt for success and satisfaction, sometimes coming close, but the quarry turns into a bubble, bursting at the touch. Lost and hopeless we can never make Heaven and home on our own. When we come to the end of ourselves and call for help, our

God of love is quick to hear the heart cry, is ready to receive the lost one into the good ship, Grace, and carry him to the desired haven.

Of course, two things are necessary: First, an admission and recognition of ones' lost and desperate condition. Second, complete trust in the good Captain of salvation, the Son of God, by which you accept His invitation, "Come," and get into the boat.

We worked a lot with young people: sometimes in programs focusing on crafts, like building model airplanes, or derby cars: sometimes working with a scouting program: often going on overnight or extended hikes. For fifteen years we took various age groups on extended canoe trips. Ten to twenty-five young people would travel for four to six days through a system of lakes and portages, learning wilderness survival, human relations, swimming, fishing for the always plentiful rainbow trout, and always Bible training. Our interest was more than, "Keeping the kids off the street," as the saying goes. Young men and women have a greater need than that. They need to find out the principles and standards of righteous living, learn to know God, and get settled on the spiritual reality of Heaven, and how to get there.

Along with our good co-laborers, we saw the need to purchase property for a Christian camping program. In those days of development, lands were available for such purposes from the federal government. Three of us walked the perimeters of what would later become Solid Rock Bible Camp and made the formal application to acquire that fine property which included a small lake.

We hired Morris Coursen and his caterpillar to build a road and clear ground for a lodge and playing field. Kenny Carver brought in his drilling rig for a well. An active year-round program has been carried on there since.

Later, our churches worked together to develop a camp in Homer. After some years, it was sold, and the proceeds were used to build Higher Ground Baptist Camp in the Sterling area. Again, the Lord blessed the effort. The 155-acre campus, which is still in use today, includes a large main lodge with all the facilities, first rate bathhouses, several sleeping cabins and a nice director's home. Retreats and camper weeks run throughout the year.

Main street Soldotna – 1959

Beginning in Soldotna

CHAPTER 5

It's a Flying North

Airplanes were and still are a necessary part of Alaskan life. The road system is good, but limited, leaving many towns and villages in a vast and wild land inaccessible by road. Flying had never been of interest to me until our first year in the country demonstrated its value.

There were always small commercial airplanes to carry you about anywhere you could think of going, but such charter service was prohibitive cost wise. I began to think and pray about flying lessons, but was ignorant of costs and procedures. On our first trip "Outside" to report to our supporters, I spoke in an Ohio church where I became acquainted with a friend who worked on the Mexican border. As we compared notes on our work, I casually mentioned the new interest in flying. The meetings ended and we went our separate ways.

Some weeks later we received a letter from him, inviting us to come to south Texas. A crop duster, by the name of Roy McArdle would give me his time and the use of an airplane to teach me to fly. We checked our rather full schedule and arranged two weeks for instruction. The long drive from Pennsylvania to Texas and then back again would eat up a chunk of that time, but we decided to give it a try. I'm so glad we did.

Roy and Sally McArdle owned nine airplanes in their crop dusting business, including a couple of 1929 Travel Airs and Stearmans. Roy did all the mechanic work to keep them flying, besides doing a lot of the dusting. They loved the Lord, gave heavily to missions, and were active in their local church. They treated us like family and we felt like we were!

Harlingen, Texas, served as our base and was located near the US and Mexico border. We had flown together for a day or two and I began to think secretly about visiting Mexico, however, I knew that time would not permit a trip. Nevertheless, I said to myself, "Self, if we ever solo this thing, we'll fly over and see Mexico from the air."

With about fourteen flying hours behind me, it happened. In ignorance, and without a single thought about border laws, away I flew across the Rio Grande. Flying on, I came to a small town. I dropped down to four hundred feet and circled the community, looking it over. Even from that dizzy height I was impressed with the dirt streets, apparent poverty, and crude houses. I flew the airplane back where I belonged, blissfully unaware that I had broken the laws of two nations and could have been shot down!

Not long after, Roy and I were flying the piper cub up the river toward El Paso. He was in the back seat. Leaning forward he shouted, "I feel like the Lord would have me give you this airplane!" It's a wonder I didn't spin it into the ground right then.

So it was that I returned to Harlingen in April, fueled up the airplane, and headed for Pennsylvania. I had completed the FAA written exam for a private pilot's license in Charlotte, NC, while speaking in that area. I was legal, although my logbook showed only forty hours.

I was to learn some valuable lessons on that long cross-country trip. An impersonator of Mark Twain once said, "The man that sets out to carry a cat home by the tail will learn some lessons that will always be valuable."

At the end of that first day, I landed proudly at El Campo, Texas, tied the airplane down at the edge of the grass strip, and hiked the mile into town. Early the next morning, I was back at the airplane, and untied the cub with a due measure of excitement. Carefully setting the throttle, I moved around to the nose of the plane in order to turn the prop by hand, as the plane had no starter. All true pilots can guess what happened next. The engine fired immediately. I dodged away from the spinning propeller (they kill people), grabbed a wing strut as it went by, and with great long leaps possible only to the young, I reached across the pilot's seat and chopped the throttle just before the thing was airborne.

A thousand times I have been thankful for the One who never, never leaves me (Hebrews 13:5). I've never forgotten the lesson I learned that day. No damage was done and in fifteen minutes I was flying north for Houston, happy as a kitten with a spool of thread.

Over Houston I was promptly lost! I have never liked large cities, and I didn't like Houston that day. Smog and fog pushed my craft lower and lower until the altimeter was reading four-hundred feet and forward visibility down to less than a mile. It felt like I was in school—a second or third grader trying to do Algebra.

Some will ask, "Why in the world didn't you use your radio?" The answer is very simple. There was none! That was not uncommon in those days. In Roy's fleet of nine airplanes there was not a single radio! So, I was traveling across the USA as a very inexperienced pilot with no radio.

I just kept chugging prayerfully ahead, holding a 360-degree compass heading and talking to the Good Shepherd.

Then suddenly there it was, a beautiful, black water tower with the town name printed in great large letters. I was low enough and close enough that there was absolutely no trouble reading it! Cross checking the aeronautics chart, I found my location.

It's a good thing to know where you are and where you are going—in all circumstances. Years later flying across the Midwest, I had a rather eerie feeling as I passed a radio tower extending up two-thousand feet above ground level!

Sometimes in life we find ourselves in situations with zero visibility. It is a great and blessed comfort to realize that there is one in Heaven who sees and knows our deepest care. Old Job in the middle of trials few others had known said, "He knows the way I take and when He has tried me, I shall come forth as gold." And when we are in the deep waters, He is with us and the rivers are controlled and will not overflow us (Isaiah 43:2).

If you are reading this and find that your life is a puzzle with directions as dark as night, look up. Put your trust in the Savior-Shepherd. Generic faith, that is, faith in faith, or faith that good prevails always, or faith in yourself—is rightly called pie in the sky by and by. However, faith in the Christ who lives is no dream. He is real, and He is able and willing to do what He says He will do. What He says in His word, He must do.

Somebody said, "The only thing that can forecast, fix, or force God is His own word!" A strong statement, but true. "He cannot deny Himself" (2 Timothy 2:13). He says in the Book, "I will instruct thee and teach thee in the way thou shalt go, I will guide thee with mine eye" (Psalm 32:8).

Yet another lesson or two awaited me before I would see Pennsylvania again. About 50 miles north of Greenville, Mississippi is the little town of Tutwiler. As I approached the area, the weather deteriorated rapidly. A repeated warning from my good instructor rang in my ear. "Never, never fly in a thunderstorm." So, there I was flying in a thunderstorm, praying for a place—any place—to get out of the sky, and suddenly there appeared through the now pouring-down rain a very inviting grass airstrip. It didn't take me long to make the decision to land.

As I approached lower altitudes, the ground didn't look so inviting. It appeared to be covered with high, thick grass. Deciding to punch on through the rain, I pulled up from the low inspection run. Then a bright shaft of lightening lit up the windshield—which generated an irreversible decision to get on the ground. I brought it around on a short approach and put it down. The grass was two feet high, and beneath the grass lay six to eight inches of water. There was a very, very short ground roll, an abrupt halt, and the airplane was up on its nose. A shocking first-timer for this low, low-timer.

The crop-duster who owned the strip was watching the action, and thankfully, was very good natured and kind. He quickly drove his Ford tractor to the wounded bird, righted it, and towed it to his hanger to assess the damage.

Careful inspection revealed only a bent airscoop. He gave me a bed for the night and the next morning removed the damaged part and took it somewhere for repairs. He reinstalled the scoop and called the state police for permission to take off from the highway that ran by the front of his place. Two or three patrol cars came and blocked off the stretch of road. I happily took off, noticing all the poor people who were standing on their porches watching the fun.

Two days later, I was again in bad weather, this time approaching Pittsburgh, Pennsylvania. I said to myself, "Self, let's land in Pittsburgh before things get any worse." Self agreed. So, we headed for Allegheny county airport (without radios remember). The tower flashed a green light welcoming me to land.

I made a phone call to Esther—a hundred miles north, as I was tired of the weather. She came with the car and I tied the airplane down to wait for some sunshine before flying it home. And home had very few places that would provide enough room to land it. Narrow valleys rimmed with high-timber covered hills didn't make for airfields.

A farmer friend had one large field, over which I walked, and decided that it was adequate. He gave permission. The day I arrived, while I was digging in a couple of tie down anchors, a very angry neighbor came flying up the field in his Lincoln Continental.

"Get that thing out of here!" be blasted.

I ignored him and kept on digging. He had leased the field for a crop and the owner had failed to tell either of us. We both understood soon enough that in order to prevent gunfire I had better find another field.

The old school house I had attended was about a mile east of that field. The windows of the fourth grade class faced toward that field. Anna Smith had been my fourth grade teacher and she was teaching that day I took off. She had a lot of practice scolding.

"Paul Weimer," she said, "We thought you were coming right through the window!"

I know I was six or seven hundred feet high, but I also knew better than to contradict her.

Salmon drying in village

Grandson Micah – Kodiak Island

CHAPTER 6

Soldotna

There wasn't a lot to the town of Soldotna back then. Kenai, which was ten miles away, was still kind of a fishing village. In Kenai, there were several stores but no paved roads, not to be compared with the modern development there now. It was obvious that Soldotna had a bright future as an important center on the Kenai. But there was no church of any kind in the area.

We decided to purchase two lots for $300.00—a bundle of money for us then. We acquired a used trailer house, eight by thirty-five feet, cleared the lots, and built a large lean-to providing living quarter for our growing family. The property fronted on what would later become Redoubt Avenue, but the street then was nonexistent. There were just miles of birch trees.

We hired Jess Robinson to come with his D-8 cat to put in the street—an interesting operation. After pushing the trees aside, he excavated a huge, deep hole, perhaps twenty feet down. He then pushed all the trees and brush into that hole, and covered it with the aggregate he had excavated.

This was the beginning of beautiful Redoubt Avenue that currently looks straight down towards Redoubt Volcano as one drives south.

When the well-driller hit water at 140 feet, it proved to be artesian with beautiful water coming out of the top of the well.

We immediately began planning for a church house. The season was late—into November. I had several truckloads of gravel dumped in a pile at the building site. Six fifty-gallon drums with the ends cut out and placed end to end formed a tunnel under that gravel mound. A wood fire burning in one end thawed the gravel and heated it sufficiently for the concrete mix.

Using rough lumber, I erected a crude frame over the entire building site and covered it with plastic. With some large wood stoves and a "salamander" heater inside, we were ready. In November the walls were poured. Through December and into March we roofed it, insulated it, poured the floor and prepared for meetings.

Rough as it was, people came. The first to accept Christ was a young mother named Dot who continued to be a dear friend for many years, even after moving out of Alaska to New York state.

One day Dot said, with a smile, "I'd like to join this church."

I asked, "Have you received the Lord Jesus as your Savior?"

She had been a member of a liberal church, but had never been confronted with that all-important issue. I explained briefly how one becomes a real Christian (John 1:12). She went home and the following week, there in her new kitchen, she called on the Lord for salvation. Today she is in Heaven, having lived and served for many years, a faithful Christian testimony.

We purchased a pre-cut 32' X 60' building out of Tacoma,

Washington, for the main floor of the church house. Fellow missionaries came from other towns and spent two weeks working with us on its construction.

One day as we worked up high on the steep roof, Mrs. Anderson flew into the yard below in her new pick-up. Quite alarmed, she insisted that I come to her house a half-mile away. Andy came over from their store and she poured our cups full of coffee while he began his story.

They had started their grocery store a year earlier, literally doing all the work with their own hands, first constructing a sizable building. They purchased a truck which Andy would drive to Anchorage, 150 miles away, fill it with groceries and return to Soldotna to stock their shelves. Once each week he made the trip. He was physically strong, able to load a drum of fuel (about 450 pounds) on a pick-up truck alone.

That week, he had flown to Anchorage on business. It was all routine. On the return flight, he was suddenly, terribly shaken. There was no physically apparent reason for such alarming fear, but he could not escape the reality of it. Everything appeared normal—the weather, the airplane, but there was this persistent, new, awesome realization of God and his own mortality. Now, two days later, sitting there across the table, he was shaking so that he could not raise that cup of coffee to his lips. With a breaking voice he asked how he could be right. Prayerfully I explained from the Bible the way to peace with God, pointing out his need to surrender and trust Christ, the only mediator between God and man (1 Timothy 2:5). I was not able to persuade him.

Within a week Andy had a serious heart attack, completely unexpected. He was flown to a hospital in Portland, Oregon. I called him there, but was still unsuccessful in persuading him to surrender to Christ. He died there. Not long after, it was disappointing to receive a letter from a Portland pastor, stating that I had been too demanding and too insistent that my friend surrender to Christ, and that I should have done more before he went out. I am certain that his sudden fear on that airplane was a warning from Heaven.

When you have a genuine interest in and love for a person, you will naturally try not to offend him. However, you do him no favor by allowing him to think that he is all-right if he is not. You may choose to ride the middle of the road, fail to be clear, or shade the declarative demands God makes in His word, making it gray instead of black or white. But you cannot be true to God the judge by shading His truth.

You are no true help to your friend by comforting him, causing him to think that he is OK in his wrongs, and that he should not be overly concerned about his relationship to God.

"Thou shalt not hate thy brother within thy heart; thou shalt in any wise rebuke thy neighbor and not suffer sin upon him."

Leviticus 19:17

Paul wrote to Timothy, "Reprove, rebuke, exhort with all long-suffering and doctrine."

Our man-centered philosophies have produced churches, para-church organizations and preachers who seem unable or unwilling to stand firm on many of the truths of God. The word is *compromise*—perhaps acceptable in politics, but deplorable in handling God's revelation. We need more people who practice the Elisha mode, "Thus saith the Lord." It is a great crime against a person to declare safety when they are in great danger, depriving him of the opportunity of escape. Jeremiah, the prophet, condemned the apostates of his day as those who "heal the hurt of my people slightly saying, 'Peace, Peace,' when there is no peace." It is bad enough for you to deceive yourself; it is twice as bad to deceive another.

The popular philosophy now is to blur the truth. Make everything the same. Build a generic religion. Erase all differences. Speak proudly of values, but do not define them. Whether nationality, patriotism, religion, virtue, morality or religion—make it all the same so everybody is A-OK.

This ambivalence bug has bitten the body of Christ, a sort of spiritual arbitration, a pluralism wherein a person says he believes the Bible to be the unchangeable word of the living God, but then writes over it his own ideas, making the word fit his notions. And if his conclusions differ from those historically accepted, he will say, "Oh, it's all a matter of interpretation!" As though God's truth is subject to our fallible opinion. Sometimes this approach may be the result of a preachers desire to reach as many people as he can. So, not wanting to offend any, he cultivates an atmosphere of increasing fog and makes sugared Jell-O of eternal truth. If he perceives that some particular Bible teaching is too particular and may be divisive, why, just minimize it!

They say that insanity in America has greatly diminished, because what used to be crazy is now normal! And so it is with Generic Christianity. Believe whatever you want to— just don't act like it.

A middle-aged couple stopped on the sidewalk and said, "We're so glad to see a church in this area! We have been looking for a church that doesn't preach any doctrine!" They correctly assumed that doctrine is divisive! All God's teachings of righteousness are divisive.

One of those personalized license plates expressed it well with the letters "WTEVER". It is possible to confuse an open mind for a vacant one. The question calling for answers are: Did the Creator put something in the instruction book that is unimportant? Is the omniscient God able to record His teachings (Doctrine) in languages understandable to us? Then, finally, are we willing to exercise the discipline of searching the scriptures daily whether these things are so? Or, instead, do we prefer religious sugared Jell-O.

Truth, by nature is absolute, not relative. It is neither obsolete. It is permanent, not temporary; universal, not local; and light, not dusk. Bring your brains to the Bible and take your brains to church.

High up on the side of a mountain, I set out to cross a snow chute, about a hundred feet across. It looked innocent enough on that pleasant, late summer day. The settled, packed snow was workable, and by carefully planting each step I was making good progress. Then half way across, I slipped.

Sliding down, I noticed that there was no immediate danger. Actually it was fun, till it became obvious that my speed of decent was rapidly accelerating. Then I looked. The chute took a sharp turn down near the bottom. Things were beginning to blur with the speed. I must have been doing 500 mph! (Plus or minus.) Then, ahead of me appeared an outcropping rock from the far side of the chute.

Rolling and sliding I said, "Foot, get over there." And foot found solid rock. The accelerated slippage ceased.

This mind that considers doctrine to be unimportant and that all varying distinctions should be amalgamated under one umbrella of Christian brotherhood guarantees a toboggan slide to darkness. The pluralism that blends incompatible beliefs into one view of Christianity asks us, "When we stand before God, will He care about all these doctrinal differences?"

The answer is, "YES!"

Yes, because He gave us His book of instructions. He has "magnified His word above all His name" (Psalm 138:3). Anything that was important enough to include in His word will demand our accountability at the judgment.

Our job is not so much to make people feel good or to

build a mega-church. Rather, it is to raise the banner of truth. We must point the way to the solid rock, Christ Jesus, so that those sliding toward the precipice can avail themselves of the anchorage.

Caribou

Clam digging

CHAPTER 7

Hunting and Fishing for Men

The two men on the bank of a remote river appeared friendly enough as we visited that day. The older man was visiting from Wales. The other was his Alaskan fishing guide. As our conversation approached the subject of God, the guide went berserk and wild with anger.

He yelled and paced the gravel bar, then completed his blasphemous diatribe with a shout, "I'm as good as Jesus Christ, and if I ever see him, I will tell him so!" I could hardly believe what I was hearing! Should I give answer or challenge? Sharp tongues and dull minds often go together!

He was obviously past my help, but what about his Welsh client who had stood there quietly watching and listening. What did he know of God, whose reality was evident in the marvelous creation that surrounded us? We are advised in the Book of Wisdom, "Answer a fool according to his folly (i.e. rebuke him) lest he be wise in his own conceit." (Proverbs 26:4) So, I simply leveled with him and said, "If you see Jesus Christ, you will be on your face in the dirt." And so our relationship, which had so recently begun, came to an abrupt end as he walked away.

The black hatred that darkens the hearts of sinful men and women demonstrates with clarity the sinner's inner rebellion against his creator. "Know thyself" is good advice, though few of us do. Pride, the religion of the big "I", gets in the way, and is cultivated and fertilized with the panacea of the age, self-esteem. One would think that it would cure every social problem, even making criminals good. How strange it is that men would rather hate or ignore the best man who ever lived and belittle the Son of God who gave His own life in a horrible death on their behalf. Who ever rose from death by one's own power? Or who can so change a bad person into a good one like the Lord does when He takes up residence in the heart.

> If I buy an auto, or house, or cat
> Or put my money in this or that,
> I'd rather any day deal with the man
> Who knows his God and lives His plan.
> I'd rather my boys and girls are taught
> By men whose God controls their thought.
> I want the governor who runs the state
> To hold a principle higher than fate.
> The surgeon can better handle the knife
> Who sees in God the gift of life.
> The prominent judge whose trying your case
> Needs wisdom from the God of grace.
> You want the man who enforces the laws
> To know that God can see his flaws.
> If fixing my taxes, or lunch, or brakes,
> God's man is not led by what he takes.
> If dealing with many or just with you
> His faith in God will keep him true.
> We're better by far as we walk this sod
> When men and women believe in God.

My brother Ray (alias "Jay Bird") has always loved wild life and hunting whatever needed to be hunted. Deer, turkeys, bear and other critters of the hills of Pennsylvania had all gotten acquainted with him. When he decided to have an Alaskan hunt added, we arranged a safari. We would hunt sheep. The airplane would take us to a lake from which there was access across two drainages. The 2000 feet steep climb up to a high saddle fell away to a large bowl where we hoped to make contact, a distance of seven or eight miles.

We finally arrived in the afternoon to a spot overlooking the area where our sheep were waiting. A band of white snowballs was feeding in a high mountain meadow. We each took one, boned them out, and packed the meat, capes, and horns for the long hike back to the lake.

By that time, the light was beginning to fade, so we decided to spend the night up there, without tent or sleeping bag, and nothing to eat. As we hiked up the saddle, we noticed a small lake off to our left that would provide fresh water, and we decided to camp there for the night.

It was a surprised delight to find behind a large rock an old rusted and ragged tent, along with some tattered visqueen. With some effort, we were able to get it together, providing a little shelter on a cold mountain. Scouring the area more carefully, we discovered some old, rusted military rations beneath the rocks of a narrow defile. These were soldiers provisions issued in World War II, a variety of meals packed in small tin containers. We were starving! A sharp knife cut the lids off the rusted cans, clean on the inside! No telling how long they had rested there waiting for us. We feasted with mock thanksgiving. I think it was Mark Twain who said, "It's a terrible death to be talked to death." To be starved to death would be nearly as bad.

The next morning we were up early. We refolded and cashed our borrowed camp, loaded our packs and headed up the saddle. Climbing that 2000-ft ridge was difficult going in, but now with heavy loads, the descent was precarious. "Jay Bird" slipped on a rock face once, but the fall did no damage, other than a bent pack frame. It was a long and tiring hike, but we did reach our lake and survived to hunt sheep once again.

I have often wondered how a hunter can be so miserable in the cold and rain, with back-breaking loads, and yet be so anxious to do it all over again at the next opportunity. His wife wonders also!

A building project that fall had prevented any successful moose hunting, and we were in need of meat. Our kids were raised on wild game and it was rare for us to buy meat.

That year there was a winter hunt, so Kermit Dowse and I decided to hunt the Kasilof River country. The area we had chosen was not yet settled and held a lot of good moose habitat. We made our way over to a trail several miles up the river where there were many tracks in the snow that looked promising. I climbed a small hill, perhaps a hundred feet high that afforded a good view around the large area. Soon after, a moose appeared about 400 yards away.

I sat down and leveled the telescope sight on him and waited for him to turn his head there in the brush so I could determine whether he had horns and whether he was legal to shoot. Then a man began to yell at me. I had not seen him below me, but he was close to being in line between the moose and me. He had no idea the moose was there and it looked to him as though the rifle was pointed at him, although in fact, the line of sight was about a hundred feet over his head and to one side.

I continued quietly holding my position, determined to keep my eye on that moose until he turned his head. While he was much closer to the hunter than to me, he could not see him.

The yelling increased to desperation, then anger, as I grew just a little amused, even enjoying the situation. (Our judgment often depends on our point of view!)

The hunter's anger translated to action as he judged the guy on the hill to be an idiot about to shoot him! I heard him stomping up the hill behind me; I did not turn or rise, but kept my eye on the moose while I said, "Do you see that moose over there?" His demeanor suddenly changed when he got a clear look at the whole situation. He was hunting with a pistol, and at that distance could not consider a shot. About then, the bull turned his head. I was ready, and I squeezed the trigger when he flashed his horns. My new friend exalted in the shot, and helped Kermit and me pack out the meat.

So often we judge a person because we are near sighted, failing to see the whole picture. We are called upon to "Judge righteous Judgment." Things are not always what they seem to us. Some of the fruits of the spirit in Galatians chapter five, such as longsuffering and meekness, cannot be exercised unless you have someone around who needs your longsuffering or meekness.

Jack Lounsbury was a very colorful person with a rough past. You didn't go to sleep with him around, for there was no predicting what he would do. He and Shirley brought the family up to Alaska from Bakersfield, California, where he went to work in the new oil patch on the Kenai Peninsula.

After they trusted Christ, they became very faithful to the work. Jack was not afraid to try the outlandish and unexpected. In fact, it magnetized him. He acquired some goats and a few cows for his homestead. He traveled to Nebraska where he purchased an antique fire truck, drove it cross-country to Seattle, and loaded it on a ship bound for Alaska.

He once decided that he needed a stock buzzer for his small herd. It's a tool that resembles a large five cell flash-light, except that in place of a light bulb on one end it has an electric conductor that delivers a healthy shock to the cattle when appropriate. The day it arrived at the post office, Jack and Shirley drove to our house and put it together in the front room. Our cat was peacefully sleeping on the hassock, and Jack figured that that was just the place to test the stock buzzer. When he touched it to the tail of our sleeping cat everything changed. How that cat climbed the curtain in a flash, crossed the ceiling, came down the opposite wall and hit the backdoor I will never know. Ever after, if Jack and Shirley were to drive into the driveway, that cat was gone. I don't know if he ever slept well again.

I was stopped at a well-known business place when the owner came to the car and asked me to meet him behind the building. He had everything a heart could wish for, including the nicest home in town, a beautiful family, cars and trucks, and an airplane—success. Yet, that day, behind his business, he was deeply troubled. Like so many others, he sensed that something of great importance was missing. A person may speak impressively, appearing to be very successful, be respected and well thought of yet know that in his soul all is not well. Like the traveler who awakened with a road sign. He had been making good time, enjoying the trip and anticipating good prospects. The sign surprised him. "Danger, freeway ends."

Jesus' story of the rich fool in Luke 12 is often repeated. It was being re-enacted with HR that day behind his place of business. There, he listened carefully to the gospel of God's grace, and again later in the living room of his comfortable home. He attended our church services once or twice. Then I didn't see him anymore.

Some while later, I was again at his business establishment and asked him why he had stopped. He answered with his eyes to the ground, "It didn't work."

I asked, "Why? Did God fail to keep His promise?"

He answered, still looking down, "I guess it is my fault."

The cost was too high. The demands of Christ are high, involving a cross and dying to self (Luke14). He sold the business, moved out of Alaska, and I lost track of him. Jesus taught us to sit down and count the cost before we start building, and that if we would find the fullness of life and life eternal, He must be priority one. He will own the house he occupies; He does not use rentals.

"Whosoever he be of you that forsaketh not all that he hath cannot be my disciple." If his heart is empty of the Savior, the rich man is a pauper.

"Thou shalt love the Lord thy God" with all you are and have, is a precept of both the Old and New Testaments. We are in need of remembering that our eternal God does not change. In His very being, He is immutable so that what He was in Genesis or Deuteronomy He is today. He was holy then; He is holy now. He had standards for His people then; He has standards for His people today. We are not under His dispensation of law. Since Jesus paid our sin debt, we are under grace. But it is possible to so emphasize the grace of God that we forget and minimize his holiness.

Paul writes that we are married to Christ (Romans 7), and under the law of Christ (1 Corinthians 9:21), serving in newness of the Spirit and not the oldness of the letter.

Sometimes the conscientious follower of Jesus Christ is accused of legalism because there are things he will not do. There is an important difference. The legalist is one who believes he can be saved by his own works and by conforming to a set of rules. It is not legalism, however, for a loving child, understanding his father's wishes, to try to please his father and keep his standards.

So the true Christian has this affinity toward his Heavenly Father, created by the indwelling Spirit of Christ that governs speech and action.

Jesus said, "If you love me, keep my commandments." Simply stated, please God and enjoy His blessing. Disobey and forfeit His blessing. Lose His blessings and you lose everything. Leave licentiousness and insensibility to God with the world. You are called to be different. Salt that has lost its distinctiveness is good for nothing. The more the professing child of God loves the world and is accepted by it, the more he exposes himself to the suspicion that there is something wanting in his devotion.

Throughout church history, the people of God have been vilified, ridiculed, persecuted, burned, and martyred by a world that hated them for what they represented. The world has never been a friend to grace or holiness.

If we would want favor with the world, we would have to modify or compromise God's truth and standards. If we "Love the world, the love of the Father is not in us." "Come out and be separate" have been the watch words ever since Abraham left Ur, and Paul wrote the Corinthian church.[1]

Mt. valley strip

Mountain goat

CHAPTER 8

Drivers of Cars and Airplanes

How long has it been since your vehicle was last stuck in the mud? There was a time when it was a common experience. Pity the uninitiated, raised with pavement! You cannot appreciate improved roads and freeways until you've been stuck in the mud.

Early one April, I was cautiously making the way back on a three-mile excuse for a road that served several homesteads. We drove it regularly to pick up kids for various activities. One of the homesteaders, heading the opposite direction, was bogged down in the middle of things. I stopped and got out in the mud to help him.

Oh, the air was blue with the foulest kind of language and cursing as though he expected that to help him out of the mud! After we were able to free his rig, he thanked me and asked who I was. Ah, you should have heard the volume of apologies, and seen his face when he realized a preacher had heard his heart!

"Out of the abundance of the heart, the mouth speaks." Read Matthew 12:34-35. I told this friend that it was not my ear that counted, nor was it my name he had taken in vain. The judge of all the earth will call us to account for our words, and He knows them, even our thoughts (Psalm 139).

We have met many who have declared strongly that they believe in God, and would be offended if we called them atheists. Yet, they live and speak as though God did not exist, and He does not exist in all their thoughts. He is pronounced a fool who says in his heart there is no God. You don't have to say it with your mouth to satisfy that description, although sooner or later your mouth will describe your heart.

You have surely known one who had seemed gentle and good, suddenly turn loose a cursing, volatile tongue, exposing the evil that had lain dormant and controlled because it was convenient to appear that way. May David's desire be ours, "Let the words of my mouth and the meditations of my heart be acceptable in thy sight, oh Lord my strength and my redeemer" (Psalm 19:14). I would add, "especially when I am angry!"

A Chinook wind sometimes brings relief from sub-zero cold. If accompanied by rain, as it often is, it can make the roads a nightmare. The snow pack is turned to wet ice, slippery enough that one person can push a standing car sideways. Chains on the rear wheels alone will not keep the thing on track.

It was that kind of road on which we were traveling when we rounded a curve on an uphill grade and were confronted with a strange sight. The man's car had spun out and drifted sideways toward a twenty-foot bank. Alarmed, he grabbed a one-inch rope, tied one end to his car's bumper, crawled to the high side of the highway, and tied the other end to a tree, in time to save the car. But what about us?

His car and rope penned off the slippery road completely.

Fortunately, we saw it soon enough to slide to a stop. (By then, he was jumping around like a rooster with its head cut off. Sometimes it is hard to be methodical.) We finally got it all under control and a sanding truck came along to save our day.

The road of life is always slippery. A moment of carelessness, an act of self-indulgence, a surrender to animal appetite, can all put you in serious danger. But don't forget that someone else is traveling the same road and your slippage may mean ruin to him. We do not live to ourselves and we do not die to ourselves.

We've known a number of pilots killed in airplane accidents. Some, if not all, were very competent and not wanting in good judgment. An unexpected wind sheer in mountain terrain, a sudden engine failure, or bad weather from which there was no escape: even a couple of mid-air collisions, all fatal.

I was asked to visit a young man in a hospital who had been terribly burned. He had been working at night on an airplane over on the Kuskokwim River. The building was heated with a wood stove and he was using combustible paint. When the fumes became sufficiently strong, there was an explosion and fire. The outside temperature was fifty below zero.

Badly burned, he was able to escape the fire and get a Cessna 180 started. He flew himself one-hundred miles down river to Bethel. From there he was transported to an Anchorage hospital. Young and strong, he recovered well.

For some weeks I visited him repeatedly, explaining the Gospel and how he could be sure of Heaven, pressing him to surrender to Christ, which he politely refused.

Not long after his release, he was back flying. In the Tok area, he was to fly fuel to a remote site. They loaded a fifty-gallon drum of gasoline onto his plane; he took off, flew into a mountain and was burned to death in the fire.

We must not presume upon the grace of God. When once you have heard His wonderful plan, born of His love, that offers you everlasting life, you are then doubly responsible. The declaration, "My spirit will not always strive with man," was spoken of the degenerate society of Noah's day and the cataclysmic flood that followed. The principle applies also to our day. Warnings come for a reason. God would have you repent and turn to Him in faith while you can.

Another friend decided he wanted to learn to fly. He passed the required lessons and purchased his first airplane, a Cessna 206. Returning from Illiamna, VFR on a good day, he had come through Lake Clark Pass. As he related the story, when he came out of the pass the entire Cook Inlet Basin was fogged in. Impetuously, he flew right into the cloud, contacted Kenai radio, and expected them to direct him after getting a fix on his location.

He said, "They confused me, so I turned them off!"

He flew blindly on. After awhile he contacted Anchorage Radio. When they located him on radar, he was forty miles off course, which could easily have spelled disaster for him against a mountain. They vectored him to Anchorage International Airport.

He said, "I never saw a thing till I was a few feet off the runway."

Of course he was very fortunate, having failed to exercise the judgment to stay out of the fog. It is important to know where you want to go, how to get there, and to allow nothing that blinds you from the right course. Keep your eye on the prize, for the home in the skies!

Steve Alvine was a good friend. I remember visiting in his parent's home overlooking Kodiak harbor. At twelve years old, Steve was racing around the water below in a skiff. He grew into a fine man, became an excellent mechanic, and a good pilot, with a beautiful family.

Flying hunters back from the west-side of the island, he

encountered severe winds, which threw the airplane into a mountain. Steve was killed, a great loss.

Our friends Don Richter and Len McMillan were flying Don's 180 through Lake Clark Pass, en-route to Anchorage. Encountering clouds to the ground, they opted to do a 180 degree turn, always a good decision.

Now they were in a "white out." Don spotted a bush jutting out of the snow, giving some visual reference. But the airplane wing, lifting for the bank around, obscured the bush so they could see nothing. The opposite and lower wing struck the ground, and the airplane crashed, rolling like a ball.

Because of the poor weather conditions, it was sometime before they were rescued. I was at the hospital when the rescue helicopter landed that night. Len's face was terribly torn and ripped open, but they survived and continued to serve the Lord.

Alaska is a very beautiful and very big country. It is also very unforgiving and continues to claim many lives.

A friend was flying from Tenalian Point on Lake Clark through the pass to Kenai. He had two young people on board who had just completed a week of Christian camping. While crossing Cook Inlet, only a few minutes from landing at Kenai, they ran out of fuel. The pilot was in direct contact with the Kenai flight service, where Stan Gerlitz, whose daughter was a passenger in the airplane, was on duty. They went into the water with no survivors.

In such terribly tragic times it is only our acquaintance with the sympathizing Savior, and our hope in His promises that provide the stability and strength needed to walk on.

Drying caribou skins for mukluks (Eskimo boots of fur)

Village kids

CHAPTER 9

Earthquake

When we arrived in Alaska, we had not heard that earthquakes would be common. They were a new experience for us and I suppose one never really gets so used to it as to ignore them.

We were sound asleep in an upstairs bedroom in the middle of the night for the first one. Suddenly we were sitting up wide-awake with the distinct feeling that the bed was walking across the floor. Weird! My immediate thought went to the second coming. I asked Esther whether she had heard a trumpet. "No," she said. So I laid back and went immediately to sleep.

On Good Friday, March 1964, several of us were traveling to Homer where we were to participate in Good Friday services. The plan was for three or four preachers to speak on the seven last words of Christ. I had been assigned two fifteen-minute sessions. Esther had remained at home to care for our kids with the chicken pox. So I had caught a ride with Chuck and Rhea Reeves.

As we drove through an area of large spruce trees, the air

became filled with billowing snow. However, it was not snowing. The trees began to rock magically from one direction to another like a stiff standing choir. We had never seen anything so weird.

Our first thought was that there was a horrendous wind. Then Chuck began to have trouble controlling the station wagon. We could see the road literally roll like waves in the ocean. We were forced to stop until things leveled out.

A friend traveling in front of us with a pick-up and camper had some interesting moments. His teenage son, asleep in the camper, had just awakened and was in the process of putting on his pants. He shouted to his dad, certain he was purposely swerving the vehicle to throw him off balance.

After about a half-hour, we arrived in Homer to find Pastor Jack Cooper holding his thumb over a ruptured oil line that fed his furnace. Somehow, in the confusion, it did not occur to us to aid him in his distress, an oversight he never let us forget.

The service at the church began on time. I recall two things about that meeting, although neither had anything to do with the excellent messages. One was that large philodendron that stood in front of the platform. Each time there was an aftershock (and there were many), that thing would shake, capturing every eye. Few paid much attention to our carefully planned messages.

The other memorable thing happened when about halfway through the service, the door burst open, a stranger walked part way down the aisle and declared that the whole town was being evacuated, for a tidal wave was about to wipe it out. We did not deliberate, but joined the crowd making tracks up the hill. It turned out that the tsunami was barely noticeable in Homer—I was told it was about six inches high at the beach.

Other coastal towns were devastated. Imagine the rush

and force of waters that washed a railroad diesel locomotive off the tracks on its side. Fifty-foot boats washed half a mile inland; concrete highway and railroad bridges collapsed and gone; devastation was everywhere from a force and power beyond describing.

But as the saying goes, "You ain't seen nothing yet." The day is coming when men will go into the holes of the earth for fear of the Lord ... when He will begin, "To shake terribly the earth" (Isaiah 2:19).

The Lord Jesus predicted an increase of earthquakes in Matthew 24:7.

The book of Revelation speaks of at least five quakes that will occur during the Great Tribulation period, claiming the lives of thousands, and a major earthquake surpassing any other in all history. How foolish to place all our hopes and investments in a shaking world!

Terra Firma is really not very "Firma!" People of faith are looking for a city which has foundations, whose builder, and maker is God (Hebrews 11:10).

The morning after the big quake, I was in the grocery store talking with the proprietor. He was smiling over his good fortune of survival and said, "Well, I guess it just wasn't the old man's time for us yet!"

How very crude! It is strange how some claim to believe in God Almighty while they speak of Him in irreverent sacrilege. The evidence of experienced grace is graciousness. The proof of grace in your heart will be grace in your tongue. If you do revere our great God, then be reverent in speech and life.

Eskimo friends

Levelock – V.B.S.

CHAPTER 10

Tests

W e speak proudly of these times as the information age. We have become puffed up with our knowledge and education. Ready access via television and computer gives far more facts than we can assimilate or use.

More than a hundred years ago, a wise man said, "We ought to get a society together for the suppression of useless knowledge." I wonder what he would say today?

Paul spoke of those, "Ever learning and never able to come to the knowledge of the truth" (2 Timothy 3:7). Knowledge and the accumulation of facts do not equal wisdom. The Book of Wisdom repeatedly teaches that the fear of the Lord is the beginning of wisdom.

Scores of desperate people, finding themselves in trying situations have called the preacher they never met, in the church they never had time to attend, searching for help. They have this deep, inescapable sense that this high and holy God exists, and that some day they will have to have a good relationship with Him.

Yet their religion is sort of a spare tire arrangement. You

know how it is. Your car certainly needs a spare tire, tucked back there out of the way. You haven't even checked on its condition for quite awhile. You hope you will not need it today. It's for emergency use only. God will not be so used. True faith practices the presence of God.

Jesus said, "My sheep hear my voice and I know them and they follow me" (John 10). Wisdom understands that it is not in man who walks to direct his steps.

Sometimes, or often, our troubles are self-inflicted. The day dawns with hope and anticipation of some new adventure, then because of our thoughtlessness or stupidity, it turns into misadventure.

My friend, Marvin Moser, and I landed on a remote ocean beach to spend a night or two. Winds and high tides were often a problem, so to prepare for the worst, we cleared away driftwood and made a safe place to tie down the airplane.

Later, when we were ready to leave for home, I hurriedly cleared the area, cranked the engine for warm up, and applied power into the very brisk wind, forgetting the soft sand. Instantly the flying contraption was up on its nose with five inches of one end of the propeller bent ninety degrees. We were two-hundred miles from help.

> If you think you have troubles as big as my own
> I'm forced to admit that it's true.
> But consider the fact that mine happen to me
> While yours merely happen to you!

I found a wrench and removed the propeller. I then located two large rocks there on the beach, of suitable size and shape, placed the end of the prop between, and bent it back close to where it was supposed to be. With my single-bitted ax I carefully hammered it until we were satisfied it was straight. We proceeded to fly six hours back to home base, through poor weather, and without a shudder!

Dr. Ken Brown has been a professor of languages at several Bible colleges. We became good friends as he traveled to Alaska on speaking tours and hunting trips. On an occasion, he brought a friend, Randy Allender, from San Francisco, and I agreed to fly them in search of moose. (In those days it was legal to fly and shoot the same day, a practice greatly abused and later outlawed.)

On that trip, the plan was to fly around and possibly find a legal animal within a mile or so from a possible landing area, make a stalk, and if successful, carry the meat to the airplane. We had been in the air for a couple of hours when we located three or four moose reasonably close to an old airstrip.

What looked like a perfectly easy arrangement was to turn into one of those misadventures. By the time the pilot was finished with the landing, there was a ground loop, a wing tip was mangled, and the fuselage so twisted that the tail wheel was pointing heavenward instead of ground-ward.

After awhile a Super Cub flew over, spotted us and dropped a note which read, "If you need help, stand out on the runway."

It was obvious enough that we needed help! We stood out on the runway, waiting for him to come in and land. But, no … for some strange reason known only to him, he did not land, but instead, radioed air rescue. Then it made radio news reports that there had been an accident with possible fatalities!

Our information age is sometimes blighted with false or exaggerated information and the confusion with which it keeps company. Anyhow, after two or three hours, a great military helicopter arrived to transport us home.

Now the question was, "How do we retrieve the airplane from the bushes?"

My friend, Mel Wick heard the news and was soon on the

telephone. He said, "I'll have it ready to fly out of there in twenty-four hours!"

I said, "How? You haven't even seen the wreck!"

He answered, "What did I say?"

Bud Lefstedt flew us back to the site with parts and tools, and Mel, the magician, went to work. After stripping all the fabric off the fuselage, he began cutting, bending, and fixing the tubing that made up the frame until all was straight again, and the tail wheel pointed back to the ground. We covered the entire fuselage with duct tape, taped up the mangled wing tip, and she was ready to go in twenty-three hours!

Mel said, "I just made a calculated guess on the trim setting, so you'll need to be careful and perhaps add pressure to the controls to compensate for any error."

Of course, I made it back to my airfield without further incident. When I taxied up, employers from the repair shops on the field came out to ask me who had done the work. They wanted to hire Mel on the spot! But he considered it routine. It's an understatement to say he could fix airplanes, but HE COULD FIX AIRPLANES!

Perhaps you have heard the old euphemism of dedicated Christians, that "he's so heavenly minded he's no earthly good." It is a delight to see the contradiction of that in practice. There are many that love the Lord while exercising some very practical gift, well sharpened. Come to think of it, I have yet to meet one who is so heavenly minded he is no earthly good. Though I have met some so earthly minded they are no earthly or heavenly good!

Paul with a silver

Food cache

CHAPTER 11

The Spirit of God and Other Spirits

To clear ground for the construction of a new building, we had to cut and carry away a considerable amount of brush and trees. While several of us were busy with the job, I noticed one of the men talking to a well-dressed stranger across the lot.

Before long my friend came over and said, "Pastor, you'd better come and talk to that man there." I walked over and greeted him, but my smile soon faded, when he asked, "What are you doing to the trees?"

Now, I thought maybe this guy was a government inspector of some kind. My response was brief, "Huh? We are cutting them!"

He said again, "What are you doing? Why are you cutting them?"

Sure enough, I thought, here's another inspector. I never could keep up with all of them. Seems they've proliferated like termites, though perhaps more useful. I pointed him to the construction permit we had posted, explaining that we were building a church house, that we had fulfilled all legal requirements, and had all the required permits.

His answer startled me, "You are hurting the trees!"

"What? Hurting the trees?" I echoed.

I have cut many thousands of them and have never heard a single one complain! Then a light came on that showed me where this man was coming from.

I said, "Oh, you must belong to one of those weird mystic religions that believe there is some sort of indefinable spirit running through plants and trees and cows? I suppose it would gag you to call him God?"

I was running short on patience when he said, "I am a scientist with a lab downtown and I can create life in my lab!"

With all the finesse of a cat—D9 that is—I said as plain as I could, "You are a liar!"

"NO," he repeated, "I can create life!"

So I repeated, "You are a liar, for if you could create life you would be the richest man in America."

I gave him an invitation but never saw him again. The lot got cleared and the church house was completed.

Effect and Cause

That cloth on the table was beautifully done;
Crocheted with care, a lovely fabrication,
For the working one well-earned admiration;
Keen mind to plan and design such production;
Precise hands to carry out the construction;
Could chance accidental explain what was done?
Or was there a mind behind its creation?

The tree in our yard is marvelously done;
A living thing that reproduces its own;
A wonderful factory built for production;

Vessels within transport its nutrition.
Leaves with trap doors that open to oxygen—
Combining it all in intricate action.
Making an apple to suit my sensation!

If the cloth on the table speaks of reason;
If the house you live in speaks of volition;
If mind is required for organization;
If daylight and dark are in regulation;
If laws of "nature" are in operation;
Can we think its all-mindless evolution?
Or is the Great God behind all the action?

Alcohol. So many lives are ruined, destroyed physically, socially and eternally by this scourge. I saw its devastation as a young teen-age boy, carrying home on the crossbars of my bicycle a drunken man unable to walk. I decided early on that I did not need booze.

Joe's trailer house was located about five-hundred yards from ours. We had become friends over the previous year. Their kids came to our Sunday School and mom and dad came often to the services.

Joe had not accepted Christ. He was a big man, about six feet tall, mild mannered, quiet, and friendly. He had moved his family to town from Northwest Alaska.

This particular mid-winter night was chilly with a thermometer reading zero degrees Fahrenheit. We never locked our front door in those days. Late that night, around 2:00 A.M. the squeaking of our front room rocking chair awakened us. I was interested to know who had found comfort in that chair. So, I quietly ventured out for a look.

She was completely naked except for a little child's open sweater and had walked barefoot through the bitter cold to find shelter in our house. Esther was soon up to bring suitable clothes and brew a pot of coffee.

The story that night was tragic, and would later have a more tragic end. Her well-mannered husband had been drinking and began to beat his wife. So, she had escaped to our house. We waited until morning before going to the house, where I found Joe in a drunken stupor.

A year went by. While we were out of state on a speaking tour, he got drunk again, and again beat his wife—this time killing her. From prison, Joe wrote me several times, seeking help to gain release. Much later, I was able to visit him in prison. He claimed to have received the Lord, but his life, his family, and the lives of his children were all ruined over alcohol.

On another late night the road was dry, straight, and wide. Ahead, my headlights picked out two or three vehicles stopped in the road at different angles, and a body lying in the road. While others arrived to examine her, I looked away over in the brush a hundred yards to another car with its headlights still on. When I opened the driver's door, a well-dressed gentleman said just one sentence, "Never drink and drive!" He seemed unhurt, but had learned a lesson too late.

The temperature was around ten above at 4:00 AM. Rounding a curve, I could see in the headlights a body lying motionless in the middle of the road, a major highway. I stopped within five feet, the man did not move. I assumed he was dead. I found him to be a young man, perhaps thirty.

When I reached to lift him, he asked, "What are you doing?"

I said, "You have to get out of the middle of this road, a truck rounding that corner would kill you before he could stop!"

He said, "Leave me alone! I'm sleepy!"

Of course he was drunk, and after I dragged him off the road, he lay right down and went back to sleep. He survived, probably because of all the antifreeze in him.

Again, a well-dressed man in a gray business suit, entered

my back door about one o'clock in the morning. By the time I reached the kitchen entry he was starting to undress.

"What are you doing here?" I asked.

His words were badly slurred, "I'm going to bed!"

He was totally oblivious to his condition or location.

We continue to glorify alcohol, even though we know it is a terrible social scourge.

A few years back, a major radio network in one of their popular commentary programs, actually broadcast that red wine is good for our health and helps prevent heart disease.

What they did not say was that in France, the mortality rate from alcoholism and cirrhosis of the liver is twice that in America.

One-hundred-thousand souls die each year from alcohol, and we suffer nearly ninety-billion dollars in economic damage annually. We excuse it, first by claiming to control it with moderation, or failing that, we call it a disease—curable only by a psychologist.

As someone has pointed out, if it is a disease, it is the only disease that bars the sick from heaven (I Corinthians 6:10).

- It is the only disease contracted by an act of the will.
- It is the only disease requiring a license to sell.
- It is the only disease earning profit for the sales people.
- It is the only disease producing revenue for the government.
- It is the only disease no germ or virus can cause.
- Nearly one-half of spousal abuse cases are caused by it.
- 90% of men in the Alaska domestic violence program are servants of it.
- 90% of abusive parents use it.
- 64% of criminal homicides involve alcohol.

- 56% of violent offenses involve it.
- 72% of rapes are results of it.

All alcohol related.

> One evening in October, when I was far from
>   sober,
> And dragging home a load with manly pride,
> My poor feet began to stutter, so I lay down in
>   the gutter,
> And a pig came by and parked right by my side.
> Then I warbled, "It's fair weather when good
>   fellows get together."
> A lady passing by was heard to say,
> "You can tell a man who boozes by the company
>   he chooses!"
> Then the pig got up and slowly walked away.[1]

Of course, there is a successful, wonderful deliverance for any person who will receive it. "The blood of Jesus Christ, God's son, cleanses us from all sin" (1 John 1:7).

Alcohol is included in the "Old things, all things," description of the true convert to Christ. "Old things are passed away, all things are become new" (2 Corinthians 5:17).

CHAPTER 12

Flying Is ...

The airplane magazine advertisement read, "Flying is aptitude, altitude, and attitude." That is an important and accurate three-word instruction for controlling the airplane so that it carries you to the desired destination without shipwreck. They are also fitting words for the way you conduct your life.

Aptitude: We had none that was native to us. The repeated indictment in God's Book is that there is none that seeks God or does good. One may argue against that if the subject is his relationship and reputation before other humans. However, when measured against the infinite holiness of God, "They that are in the flesh cannot please God" (Romans 8:8). We are defined to be dead in trespasses and sins, and therefore unable and unwilling to know God and His will, or to perform it.

Altitude: We are earth-bound by nature, we "mind earthly things," and we are without any real knowledge of Heaven, Heavenly things, or any objective prospect of going there. The second chapter of Ephesians describes our earth-bound existence as, "having no hope and without God in the world."

Attitude: We by nature are tilted and headed in the wrong direction. Bent and inclined toward sin, headed downward, not up. Indeed, flying blindly toward eternity and unable to reach God. Powerless. Dead.

It is frightening to be caught in a strong down-draft in mountainous terrain, when the application of full power to the oversized engine is insufficient to gain altitude. It describes our spiritual self-effort. As Paul wrote, "When I would do right, evil is present with me."

However, everything changes wonderfully when the Lord Christ is the pilot.

> Once I was wandering, alone in my sin;
> I had no happiness, no freedom within.
> Then Jesus came to me. Set my spirit free.
> Now I am rejoicing, there's been a change in me![1]
> (Therron Babcock)

Aptitude: He's no longer unschooled or a stranger to spiritual truth. The Spirit of God who now lives within him, teaches him. Things in the Bible he could not understand before, things that previously held no interest, but were like a foreign language, he now begins to comprehend. The light has been turned on. He is an eager student of eternal truths and values. He has what John called an unction or an anointing (1 John 2:20). He can understand things which before held no meaning.

Altitude: He continues to climb. His home is in Heaven, from where he looks for the Savior. His actions, interests, speech, and aspirations move now on a higher plane.

Like the early spring plant in the window, he turns toward the sunlight of God and His Word. For, now he has a new nature within that reaches for heavenly things. He presses for the mark of the high calling of God in Christ Jesus. Before Christ (BC) he could not follow the Good Shepherd on the journey, or expect to live in Heaven at the end of it. A safe landing at that destination was completely uncertain. Before Christ came in, his whole inclination was to satisfy the desires and appetites of his own self. Me first and capital I.

Now he is regenerated, under new management, magnetized to a new force. He desires that the words of his mouth and meditations of his heart be acceptable to his watching God, his Strength, and his Redeemer. He has surrendered the controls to his Instructor. His guiding principle is now, "Search me, oh God, and know my heart: Try me and know my thoughts, and see if there be any wicked way in me, and lead me in the way everlasting."

To put it another way, one's lifestyle and path through life is governed by intelligent motive and discipline. The boat in motion is driven by some force: A.) It may be natural, such as tide or wind, in which case it is adrift with no certain future. B.) It may be under tow, pulled along by some outside force. C.) It may have a built in power supply, controlled by a master.

In either case it is controlled. And we are controlled, either by doing what comes of appetite and natural force, or satanic influence, or, if we are born again, by the indwelling Spirit of Christ who empowers and steers on the course leading to the safe harbor.

Did you ever meet anyone who did not want to go to Heaven when his or her life ends? I do not remember ever meeting anyone who wanted to go to Hell! What rational person wants to crash in flames at the end of the flight?

Remember Jonah? For a little bit there, he got his attitude and direction off kilter when he chose to avoid what the Lord clearly told him to do, thus moving in the wrong direction.

Now, despite Jonah's temporary loss of altitude, there are

several things about that ancient prophet I like. He believed God and stayed on speaking terms with Him. He "paid the fare," (Jonah 1:3). He was no stowaway, nor did he expect someone else to buy his ticket. He spoke the truth, even when the truth put his life in jeopardy. That's integrity!

The Bible says that one of the marks (attitude) of the person who dwells with God is that, "He swears to his own hurt and changes not," (Psalm 15:4). Jonah told the storm-driven sailors to throw him overboard into the raging sea! And there are some who can't speak the truth to their own spouse—or to the tax collector, thinking to save a few dollars.

Flying to Heaven is:

Aptitude: Jesus said, "Learn of me."

Altitude: "Set your affection on things above, not on things on the earth."

Attitude: "Take my yoke upon you."

Tustamena Lake

On the beach. Airplane lost through ice of Tustamena.

CHAPTER 13

The Long Night

G od always answers the prayers of His children. I wonder if sometimes when we ask for prayer support, we
focus on the influence we think the person praying may
have, instead of on the One whom hears and answers prayer.
Do we think that the greater and more popular Christian has
more influence and power in prayer?

In the case at hand, scores of unsolicited cries to God
ascended from loving hearts throughout a long, long night,
and God heard. It was a remarkable answer to prayer. Not
unusual, but remarkable.

Tustamena is a large, glacier-fed lake, twenty-four miles
long and six to seven miles wide on the Kenai Peninsula, fifteen miles up stream from salt water.

It was mid-April, and all the area lakes were still frozen,
with two or three feet of ice, and no water showing anywhere in a white landscape. I carefully touched the wheels
to the surface of Tustmena Lake, the ice appeared firm and
gave confidence that it was. Then suddenly the airplane
wheels found a soft, slushy area (the consistency of a glass

of crushed ice and water) which was invisible from above.

The Piper Cub lost flying speed instantly. The application of full power was insufficient to escape, and it went over on its nose in three feet of slush atop two-hundred and twenty-five feet of water, sinking. Suspended from seat and shoulder harness, the view through the windshield was that of gray-green glacier water. By the time I could free myself and exit the cabin, hauling up on the wing, I was soaked from the waist down. Quickly, I crawled back up the fuselage to the tail. My added weight there was enough to bring the tail down and level the airplane on the surface of the mush, providing greater buoyancy to keep the thing from going nose down to the bottom.

The time was two in the afternoon, and it was obvious that I was in a pretty desperate situation. My first decision was to try running across the rotting ice to the shore, three quarters of a mile away.

Walking around the perimeter of the airplane (the top of which was then nearly even with the ice), I began to test the lake's surface. The first two or three places were completely unstable. Then I found a spot off the left wing tip that would support my weight. I stood away from the airplane, and hoped that, by rushing, perhaps there would be a chance to reach shore. Two quick steps and I was swimming up to the neck in slush.

Struggling back to the wing, now level with the ice, I crawled out and took off my coveralls, boots, liners, and socks, wrung the water out as best I could with numb, freezing hands, and put them back on. There could be no escape across the ice.

With a pocketknife, I cut a hole in the top of the cabin area, reached through the three feet of ice water and retrieved the emergency-locating transmitter. Would it work, having been so submerged? I triggered it and hoped. I tried to persuade myself that the airplane would remain afloat on the surface of the slush ice, however, water crept slowly over the wings, demonstrating that it was very slowly, but surely, sinking.

The ELT transmits a sort of whining signal on an international emergency radio frequency. The technology of the satellite system enables them to catch that signal, compute the location, fix and transmit it back to earth to a rescue coordination center, from which searchers are sent out to the rescue.

A triangle similar to one in place long ago that tells the account of a Roman soldier named Cornelius. He was a devout, giving, praying man, but he was lost and doomed. He admitted his plight. His prayers went up to the God he could not see. God sent His signal down to a man named Peter. The rescuer carried the way of salvation back to Cornelius.

That triangle is still in operation. When a stranger to hope recognizes his need of salvation, God sees, and the rescue coordination center (the bible-believing church), sends out the searchers (Matthew 28:19-20). The lost one hears the way of salvation and is brought to Christ and eternal life.

Well, I waited throughout a long, cold afternoon. Shivering soon increased to uncontrollable shaking that would not stop for the next twenty hours. I dared not stand or sit long on the wings because increased weight in that area contributed to a nose down, sinking tendency. I had stayed there long enough to kick a hole in the windshield to retrieve half of a down vest floating in the cabin. It was caught on something there so I ripped it in two. I then wrung it out and put it on.

The gas tanks were located in the wings, with their filler caps on top. Desperate with cold, I irrationally tried to ignite the fuel, but not one of my waterproof matches would light.

Back on the tail surface, now also gradually sinking, I hooked one leg over a brace wire to help keep balance. With the pocketknife, I cut strips of fabric from the vertical stabilizer and stuffed them beneath my wet clothes to help shield from the bitter wind.

Several hours passed, when the unique engine drone of the Civil Air Patrol Beaver airplane came drifting across the ice. What a beautiful sound! The ELT had worked and the satellite had caught the signal. But there was a mistake some how, a skip that misinterpreted my location by eight miles or so to the northeast, up against the mountains, so that is where the search focused. I could hear them flying around up there and began to wonder about their ability to do anything right!

Considerable time elapsed as they flew in circles, until finally the Beaver came into view quickening my hope. For two hours I watched him come and go, carefully combing the shores of the lake. Once they actually flew just a few hundred feet from my position, but my airplane had settled flat into the surface of the ice, with nothing protruding but the vertical stabilizer where I stood, making it nearly invisible in the expanse of ice. They did not see my wild waving, and to my great dismay, left the area about seven o'clock in the evening.

At nine o'clock, April 17, darkness settled over the frozen lake for that long, long night.

Some of my past, hair raising, emergency situations have included angry mama bears, vertical mountain cliffs, adverse flying conditions and malignant disease that wrinkled the doctor's brow. Usually an emergency can be sweated out for a moment, handled with prayer, and afterward considered with smiling praises to the Great and Good Shepherd. But then, for twenty-one hours I was made to face the probability of death by one of two factors—neither of which was very appealing. I would either freeze to death or drown.

I planned that the last move would be to throw the locator

transmitter across the ice so it could be known where I was.

At ten o'clock, large flakes of snow began to fall on my hatless head. With my pocketknife, I fashioned a crude hat and headband from the fabric tail beside me. The wind picked up, driving all the way through my water soaked clothes. The water, now covering my perch, froze around motionless boots to three-quarters of an inch of ice.

Knowing that body movement would hasten the sinking of the airplane, I dared not exercise. The body never stopped shaking and severe cramps set into back and legs from the statue stand.

At eleven o'clock, the sky cleared to a beautiful, star filled, moonlit night. My shadow moved slowly across the surface of the submerged plane. It was impossible to stay awake. I would drop off to sleep standing straight up and shaking violently. I realized I must stay awake somehow.

On top of the vertical stabilizer there was a beacon light, about the size of a coffee cup. When sleep overcame, I would drape over that beacon, and go instantly to sleep. In less than a minute, the pain from it buried in my chest would waken me. All through the night the maneuver was repeated.

Occasionally, I could see a satellite racing across the sky beneath the stars, a moving light listening for my ELT signal. I prayed and sang and shouted. (Say, it's good to memorize Bible verses! Sooner or later you are going to need those valuable treasures in time of need.) Among the many shouted toward Heaven that night, were Isaiah 43:2, Deuteronomy 33:27, Psalm 91:10-12, and all of Psalm 139. Stop and look them up!

I found out why Job, in error, presumed to preach to God. Technicalities of context or interpretation were not important. The whole Word was mine, for me and to me, and that was the time to shout it. The closest human ears, not counting my own, were many miles away, but God was there.

The first purple hints of dawn on a clear night were beautiful and filled with hope. And soon there came another visitor.

With the dawning came a depressing fog. By full daylight it was so thick, that visibility was less than a hundred yards.

> "Why art thou cast down, oh my soul and why art thou disquieted within me? Hope thou in God, for I shall yet praise Him who is the health of my countenance and my God."
>
> *Psalm 42:11*

I reminded the Lord of the fog, just in case He hadn't noticed; and how airplanes could do no searching in such conditions; and that time, as always, was short.

For hours I had carefully examined myself to come to some judgment as to the reason for my misery. The conclusion of such deliberating was that God is good, and while he chastises His children, He does not torture them. Our tests will not be more than we can bear by His grace (1 Corinthians10:13). Nor would He hide the reason for the chastening, or leave us in ignorance of any adjustments we need to make. Once I had come to the conclusion that the source of my difficulty was of the evil one, I could intelligently pray for his defeat and for my deliverance.

Shortly after 6:00 A.M., there came that wonderful sound of a choir of airplane engines. A dozen friends, true brothers, were out there searching. I knew who they were, though I could not see them.

"But Lord," I prayed, "move this fog away before this airplane goes to the bottom of the lake with me!"

About 9:00 A.M., I heard a helicopter work up the beach from the west-end of the lake. Back and forth he flew, searching the shoreline a thousand yards from me, but the inpeneratable fog closed the door to my room. Then, very gradually, it began to thin. The dim form of trees along the beach began to appear. As the first faint rays of sunlight peeked through, the warmth was absolutely wonderful. For the first time in over twenty hours the violent exhausting shaking of my body slowed. With mixed emotions I noted that this marvelous warmth would also hasten the sinking of my plane.

At ten-thirty I heard the helicopter engine shut down. Although I could not yet see the craft, I knew he had landed on the beach. Now, any preacher worth his salt can shout. He's practiced and can cry aloud! For the next ten minutes that frozen lake heard the finest Baptist shouts ever uttered.

"Hoooo—south on the iiiiiceeee."

I could hear the echo roll along the beach for a mile. However, the two state troopers near the helicopter never heard a thing! They had become frustrated in their search and before leaving the area had decided to land and investigate a small, broken down trappers cabin in the woods just up from the beach. Finding nothing there, they returned to the helicopter and sat there eating a sandwich. Soon after, they spotted a strange object out across the ice. After studying it with binoculars for five minutes, they concluded it was a moose stuck in the ice. However, before leaving the area, they would fly out for a closer look.

It was wonderful to see that machine rise fifty-feet into the air and head directly toward me. In minutes, the helicopter skid was just a couple of feet from my sinking perch and I stepped across to safety. The troopers were amazed to see that I was OK and pointed to Heaven as if to say they knew why.

During the twenty-five mile flight to an airport, they radioed the other searchers of the rescue. Never will I forget the enormously emotional feeling of stepping out of the chopper to that circle of a dozen happy faces of dear friends. The whole experience awakened incredible emotion.

After some hot soup and coffee in a warm restaurant, I

pulled off my boots and socks to reveal feet that had turned a purplish blue as though they had been painted. They would subsequently swell to twice their normal size, reject shoes for several days, then blister and peel for three weeks. My left hand was swollen, as well, and frost bitten.

A funny thing happened when I took off that half a down filled vest. Feathers flew all over the lobby, but the restaurant folks were very kind.

Three hours from the moment of rescue, we had a Ranger Helicopter at the sight attempting to retrieve my airplane. As soon as the mechanic stood on it to attach lift lines, it began to slip into the slush. He got off just before it went to the bottom.

When the Civil Air Patrol requested that I address their eighty or so pilots on the subject of survival, I first declined. However, the man quickly said, "Oh, you can say whatever you want, even preach!"

Speaking to them at the meeting, I stated a strange fact. People are so keenly interested in the survival of the body, which is at best temporary and a mere tent, while they have little or no concern for the survival of the soul, the real self. I spoke of the Great Rescuer, the Redeemer, and Savior.

A newspaper reporter had said, "You must be in excellent physical condition!"

"NO," I replied. "I've had cancer and other things, my physical condition had little to do with this, but God answers prayer."

Someone else said, "Well, survival depends on your will to live."

Wrong again. How many I have known who had a very strong desire and will to live who died in spite of it. I guess if one's survival depended on his or her determination to live, some would live to be a thousand! Only one has the keys of death, the One above us (Revelation 1:12).

More than once I have had teams of doctors around my

hospital bed. I have looked at the strong possibility of an early death, but my times are in higher hands, and whatever He does is good. I am a survivor by His grace.

No words will ever express sufficiently the greatness and goodness of our awe-generating Savior.

I heard a teenager once speak of an "awesome" basketball player. I said, "You have used your best superlatives up on little things, now what word do you have left to describe God?"

He alone is awesome! I know why there is so much joyful singing in Heaven. It is little wonder they sing there when saved ones finally comprehend the magnitude of the rescue that happened when, "He brought me up also from an horrible pit, out of the miry clay, and set my feet upon a rock and established my goings" (Psalm 40).

> Should seven fold storms of Thunder roll
> And shake this world from pole to pole
> No thunder bolt can daunt my face
> For Jesus is my Hiding place!

Grace Baptist, Anchorage – 1970

Vacation Bible School – Grace Baptist Church

CHAPTER 14

Discriminating

Proverbs 13:20 states, "He that walks with wise men shall be wise, but a companion of fools shall be destroyed."

Be particular about your friends. Put a good apple in a bag of bad ones and guess how long it will stay good. Ben Franklin once said, "He who lies down with dogs shall rise up with fleas." It is equally true that he who has good people as true friends is greatly improved.

I suppose I have more reason than many to be thankful to count great people, good men and women, as my friends. Faces appear on the screen of memory, some now in Heaven. A good friend is a treasure indeed. How greatly Jonathan enriched David! And Abraham old Lot!

"As iron sharpens iron, so a man sharpens the countenance of his friend" (Proverbs 27:17). Sharpen a tool and you do a good service, making it more useful.

"A friend loves at all times" (Proverbs 17:17). Even when you are not at your best!

"There is a friend that sticks closer than a brother."
Proverbs 18:24

He's the same one who said, "I have called you friends and you are my friends if you do whatsoever I command you" (John 15:14).

A young man came into the Sunday evening service. He assured me he was a Christian and then asked, "May I speak to the congregation." I was young, naive, and gullible! Thinking and hoping that he meant to share a few words of testimony, I agreed. He then proceeded to ramble along for ten or fifteen minutes with this weird jumble of religious gobble-de-gook he had collected somewhere, until I finally had to stop him. One false doctrine is bad, but a string of questionable doctrine is terrible!

There are those softhearted people who chafe at confrontation, or the very idea of separation.

"Build bridges, not fences," is the nice sounding motto.

But, 1 Corinthians 15 outlines the irreducible minimums of the Gospel. You can't have anything less and still have the Gospel Truth.

a.) Christ—identify Him!
b.) Died—actually, really!
c.) For our sins—substitutionary!
d.) Buried—a well-proven death!
e.) Rose again!
f.) Scriptures—inspired of God, therefore truth, without error!

Isn't it a wonderful fact from Heaven that when one believes these truths, he or she is safe within the shelter of the love of God?

However, this Gospel is not the only thing God put in His book. True, the grand old Good News of grace that the Son

of God died to pay my sin-debt, then rose again to live forever is the best of news, suited even for a child's mind as
well as for the most intelligent. But, the Great Author of
Faith put some other desirables into His Book also, and
those who want to please their Father are careful to find out
His desires and obey His directions.

He has given explicit precepts about living regarding
things to do and things not to do. Fences. Ever notice that
most of the Ten Commandments (not 10 suggestions) are
negative? Fences!

"Build bridges, not fences," may have a catchy sound for
itching ears, but is it sound advice?

Sometimes I wonder if we should start a new organization
called "BABES"—Baptists Anonymous Believing Everything. When a church believes everything, she believes nothing. There is a place for fences as well as bridges. I want a
bridge to my neighbor's house. But I also want a fence!

Suppose you are building a house. You raise four walls,
put on a roof, and install doors and windows. Now you are
"dried in," safe—sheltered from the storms. But in northern
climes you also want some insulation, wall covering, paint,
trim, a sink or two, and water pipes and conduits for waste.
Inside plumbing is not essential to survival, believe it or not!
But, it is for cleanliness!

Electricity installed according to codes is also helpful. We
need light, and lots of it, to make it through those long winter nights. Heat. A table and a chair or two would be nice.
Plenty of amenities are not absolutely essential to survival,
but they are certainly helpful, healthy, and practical.

And a fence. Dogs and other critters have caused me
much grief over the years. I have learned that moose, though
I like them, will eat my rose bushes, mountain ash trees, and
cabbages. I will make no bridge for them, but a fence.

So the Bible erects fences. David said, "I will set no
wicked thing before my eyes" (Psalm 10:1-3).

"I have hated the congregation of evildoers, and I will not sit with the wicked."

Psalm 26:5

We are taught to avoid those who teach contrary doctrine (Romans 16:17). To separate ourselves from the ungodly and apostate (2 Corinthians 6:14-18). To withdraw from every brother who does not walk after the traditions taught in the New Testament. Traditions (2 Thessalonians 2:15 and 3:6) are the things handed down—the doctrines Paul taught.

Be particular about associates and friends. The prophet Amos asked, "Can two walk together, except they be agreed?" The answer of course is no, unless the two are willing to compromise principle and truth.

I once read of a man who, when asked what he believed replied, "I believe what my church believes."

"And what does your church believe?"

"Why, they believe the same as I believe!"

"And what do you both believe?"

"Well, we both believe the same thing!"

The danger is that we find the lowest common denominator with which no generic Christian would disagree, and make that the only important thing, disregarding all the things in the Book.

We often make our mistakes by poor judgment. And our judgment is poor because our sight is poor. So we stumble and blunder, both in the physical and spiritual world.

We landed the Piper on an uninhabited island beach just off the south tip of the Kenai Peninsula. The day was beautiful with lots of sun and hardly any wind. We enjoyed watching the otters play there in the water. However, when we were ready to leave, the airplane refused! It would not budge. The landing and roll out had been normal, but now we were in an area of very dry and very soft sand. We dug the sand away from the wheels with our hands, fired up the engine, and made a couple of feet!

Our situation grew desperate, as the tide was coming in. How we worked! Move sand, start engine, progress two to three feet, stop. How many times it was repeated I do not know. It seemed like forever!

High up on the beach where it flattened out, there was a bed of dried out kelp, perhaps forty feet wide. Grunting and straining, we aimed for it. I was sure I would die before my time! Finally, we made it, and it proved sufficient for a safe take off. It was a wonderful feeling to be airborne and headed home.

That which appears to be safe to us, even inviting, may in fact cover serious danger. Ask any mouse! The value of a trap lies in its invisibility and the value of a counterfeit lies in its likeness to the true.

Our son Nate, when he was about thirteen or fourteen years old, came hurrying into Moose Camp one day.

"Dad, I think I found some gold!"

He held out a handful of aggregate. We hurried about a quarter mile down stream to a large shallow pool. It was a pretty site with the entire bottom covered with glittering yellow flakes. How real!

"Fools gold," said the assayer. Pyrite.

And many are those who dream of and slave for the real stuff, only to discover in the end that it is vanity. Even genuine gold turns to fools gold when you have traded your life and soul for it.

I met a man who had worked seven days a week for seven full years in the oil fields, without a single day off. And of course he had no time for church or God. Seven years! He had been deceived by a counterfeit, just as surely as we have been, only with eternal consequences! Our judgment is not always good, that's why we need the Lord. He can see what we cannot see, and He always leads the right way.

On left – Don Richter's wrecked plane – Lake Clark Pass

Beach landing beside dead walrus

CHAPTER 15

Quick! Do Something!

Sometimes an emergency may arise, and develop so quickly there is no time to plan for it, or to even be afraid.

A friend hired a good and dependable pilot to land us with his Piper Cub below the foot of a glacier. We were to hike up along the edge of the glacier for a mile or so, then climb the mountain to a high and wide saddle, set up a camp, and hopefully get within shooting range of a couple of dall rams. It was an all-day hike—seven or eight hours, but fairly easy as we carried light packs.

Our pilot had airdropped most of our gear on a designated snowfield up on the saddle. We collected it all in good condition, although the carrots and cheese were all splinters from the concussion of the airdrop.

We built a shelter five by eight feet in a shallow defile, using two by twos and plastic prepared before hand. Before turning in for the night, we climbed a small hill from which we could see six or seven black bears in and around the saddle. A couple of mountain goats passed nearby, and our sheep were in sight two miles away, along the side of a canyon that paralleled our saddle.

We crawled into our sleeping bags for a good sleep, anticipating the morning. In the middle of the night the wind began to blow. And how it blew (hurricane style), threatening to blow the whole camp away! We got up in the dark and chopped squares from the muskeg, stacked it like blocks, and made a wall around our lean-to, effectively protecting us from the wind.

I heard an old pilot say, "Wind ain't no good for nuthin!"

He had lost an airplane to it once. In one windstorm twenty-five airplanes on the airstrip where ours was tied, were destroyed. Lines broken, planes turned upside down, or badly bent. Some blown away and rolled up like a ball. When you have witnessed and felt it, you can appreciate the mighty power of the one who "Gathers the wind in His fist" (Proverbs 30:4).

Bob and I were up early the next morning, headed across the saddle toward those sheep, still visible with the binoculars. We were not halfway when the excitement began. Coming up out of a shallow ravine was a mama black bear with her two little cubs, headed toward our camp.

I said, "We had better scare her away, or she will destroy our camp."

Bob was a big and strong fisherman who feared nothing. He laid his rifle down against a rock and began to walk toward the sow.

I thought, "Now why did he do that?"

Holding my rifle, I moved along with him to one side.

As we were getting pretty close, I said, "We had best not get too close for she has cubs!"

Mama bears like their cubs.

Bob said, "We'll get close enough to throw rocks at her."

And he did. He picked out a good one, about the size of a softball, threw it, and nearly hit her. She understood and she didn't like it.

Bears have a language, sometimes understood by other bears, and sometimes clear to humans as well. First she spoke to the cubs, which promptly obeyed and took off on a run down the mountain. Mama stood her ground for a moment, looking us over menacingly and snapping her white teeth. Then she began the charge. Leaping bounds, hind paws fanning her ears as she folded and unfolded directly at us.

By now she was really getting on close. I didn't want to shoot her for I was thinking of those cute little cubs. I hoped she might be bluffing and would soon stop. She didn't. If there was anything I did not want to do at that moment, it was to shoot that bear. And if there was any one thing Bob desperately wanted at that moment, it was for me to shoot that bear.

There was no place to go—not a tree to climb within three miles!

"Shoot! Shoot!" he bellowed.

Now I began to think I should, but her charge had put her in a slight depression so all I could see there for a bit was the top of her head and back. I determined that if we lived long enough for her to top out, I would shoot. The bullet cut her lower lip, entered her neck and she collapsed instantly out of a dead run.

I have been close to many bears since then, both black and brown, but never have I tried to stone one!

We went on that day and collected two beautiful dall rams—one a full curl and the other a curl and a quarter. We carried them back to our camp, cleared away some rocks, and flagged a short runway there in the saddle, where our pilot landed and ferried us off the mountain.

Village boys fishing

On the beach

CHAPTER 16

Remote

====================

It was and continues to be enjoyable to visit Alaska's many villages and the dear people who live there. Along the Kuskokwim, Yukon, and Koyukuk rivers, around Kodiak Island, and out in the Bristol Bay area, we have found many friends—and have been welcomed into many homes. These were down to earth, self-reliant, good humored people who always seemed to have time for you. The business of modern life is just starting to catch up with some. You know the philosophy, "I don't mind the rat race; I just must have a little more cheese."

Two older ladies alongside an airstrip, each with a butcher's knife, were digging in the grass.

"What are you digging?" we asked.

They only laughed.

Spotting a boy about ten, I asked him "What are they doing?"

"Come, I show you," he replied.

He took from them some small seeds, handed them to me and said, "Try them."

They were the best nuts I have ever had in Alaska! The women search the grass for a mouse's hole, dig down to the nest and rob their winter store! I never learned where the mouse got those little green seeds, but he did have good taste. I assume he carried them to the nest in his cheeks.

I once found a dead walrus on a beach, with a fine set of ivory tusks still attached. I cut them off and put them in a plastic bag in the back of the airplane. Back in Levelock, Alaska, I heated up the kitchen stove, put the head in a bucket of water to boil and so clean it up for keeping. It smelled pretty bad, but I was starting to get used to it. Then two young fellows, about seventeen or eighteen stopped by for a visit. As always, I invited them in the house.

"Eeewwww!!" they groaned. "What is that awful smell?"

I said, "You guys are real fine Eskimos, can't even stand the smell of a walrus cooking!"

They didn't stay long that day.

Bill Bursell and I left Iliamna in his Maule for Pedro Bay, a thirty-minute flight up near the head of Iliamna Lake. Bill had a Sunday afternoon Bible class in that village, a picture postcard setting with mountains rimming the lake. As we approached the ice for a ski landing in front of the village, we noticed a man and woman on the lake beside their pick-up truck, fishing through the ice. After awhile they came to the chapel where our meeting was in progress, and I met old Gilly.

"How's the fishing?" I asked.

"Oh, pretty good," responded Gilly. "Caught one-hundred-twenty-five," he said nonchalantly.

"How big?"

"Oh, a couple dozen were around twenty-five inches."

Now that is not bad trout fishing.

We were in our Bible camp dining room when one of the young women counselors came in. She had come up, along with others, from a Bible college to help us for the summer.

"Something smells good," she said. "Mmmmmm."

"It is good," I said. "It is good, want to look?"

She was skinny and hungry, so she eagerly followed me to the big stove in the kitchen.

Now, I knew that Emma Matthews, a dear Eskimo lady, was cooking four salmon heads. With a hand on the kettle cover, I enticed the young lady to get close, for it wouldn't do to keep the cover off very long and she would want a close look. I guess it was all the eyes that got to her. She left the kitchen much faster than she had entered!

I had landed on a remote beach to pour a five-gallon can of gas into the tanks. The beach was several miles long and offered a good landing sight, which ended in a wall of rock that ran out to the water. As I poured the fuel into the wing tank, a band of about five-hundred reindeer came around the end of the rock wall and stood quietly watching me from forty feet away.

The noise of the surf, and my position, rendered me totally oblivious to their presence. Emptying the can, I turned to step down and had a sudden attack of apoplexy. They were not spooked, but I certainly was! I feared they would mill along the beach preventing a take-off. However, I beat them. It's a nice feeling to outwit a critter!

As Nate and I walked along a beach, we came upon a fresh drag where something large and heavy had been pulled up across the sand after the receding tide, up a steep five foot bank, and off into the muskeg. Curious, we followed the trail a hundred yards to a large mound of muskeg, partially covering the carcass of a sea lion! Suddenly a light came on in my brain and I could imagine a great brown bear big enough to fetch that five to seven-hundred pound animal up the bank and across rough terrain. Now he would likely be close by his cache, and so were we! Our retreat was a record breaker!

Flying along the western slope of the Alaska Range, I passed over a team of dogs and their sled-riding driver. Here was a trapper, the only thing anybody could be doing in that very remote region. Turning and following his trail, I spotted his cabin on the shore of a frozen lake. A bit later, I touched the skis on the snow and taxied up to the cabin. When he arrived and had taken care of the dogs, we went inside.

The cabin was about ten by twelve feet, had a low ceiling, a dirt floor, and was cozy warm from a small wood stove. Each fall he had a pilot fly him in with his dogs and enough supplies to last through the winter. No telephone, TV, or mail delivery. He enjoyed the solitude and made his money trapping wolves, beaver, coyotes, lynx and wolverine. I was probably his only visitor for six months and we had a good visit. He listened as I shared the gospel story and gave him some good tracts, which he promised to study.

All over this great land there are people scattered like him. Others have had a dream about such wilderness living and decided to try it, but when inexperienced, do so to their great regret.

It is a big jump to the streets of Anchorage from that trapper's cabin. We had to get up close to read this bumper sticker, "People are more violently opposed to fur than to leather, because its easier to harass rich women than to harass motorcycle gangs."

The radio advertisement said, "Buy our vacuum cleaner and you will have a sweeper that will last forever!" Sure it will. Ha, ha.

There are two things about vacuum cleaners that I know for certain. First, the sweeper won't last forever. Do you suppose they exaggerate a little? There are only two things you will ever touch that are forever: your own soul and the Bible, God's eternal word. It's a great victory to get those two together!

The second thing I know about vacuum cleaners is, I do not need one that will last forever! I am going to be living in a place where nothing can enter that defiles (Revelation 21:27), and I already have the title deed (John 14:3).

"I am going to a city where the streets with gold
    are paved
Where the Tree of life is blooming and the roses
    never fade."[1]

So you see, I do not need a cleaner that will last forever.

I took some ribbing for being quick on the trigger. I say this, not because I repent of it, for I never could see any advantage in waiting and deliberating when once the quarry was sighted. Opportunity does not always linger.

I have made mistakes, both by rushing and by tarrying to deliberate. I made a terrific head shot in poor light early one morning on a wolf at two-hundred yards. My friend was also lining up for a shot, so greed had put me in somewhat of a hurry. Trouble was, when we examined the carcass of the critter, it had a collar around its neck. The large husky dog had strayed miles, far from home.

On the other hand, there was a certain dall ram. A group of hunters had made their way to the headwaters of the river and set up camp in the narrow canyon. Early the next morning we split into two groups, one party hunting on one side of the valley while three of us climbed to the top of the opposite mountain. Peering cautiously over the narrow ridge we spotted two legal rams asleep. The discussion followed. Size, distance, and most important, who should shoot first! And at which animal? Finally, my friends suggested drawing straws. How could I refuse?

I had decided long before, never to gamble, yet I generously agreed. And to my dismay, I drew the short straw. Well, it turned out that one of them connected, and the other missed. My shot was good, but it was the smaller ram. I vowed then and there to never odd-man again, and to save the discussions for the kitchen table.

There is a difference between reputation and character. Reputation is what people think you are. Character is what God and the angels think you are. I may not always be able to control the first, but I can have something to do with character. Submission to Christ, virtue, morality, meekness, kindness, humbleness, integrity, and obedience to God's word—these are my responsibility. Since I am directed to instill these into my life, it must be that I can do so with spirit-directed self-discipline.

Begiinning Dimond Blvd. Baptist Church

Dimond Blvd. Baptist Church – 2000

CHAPTER 17

Both Here and Coming

To watch the great traveling caribou herds; to climb for the mountain goat; to fish for the hungry grayling; to play the mighty King Salmon; to look a wolverine in the eyes; to watch the eagle build her nest; to wait for the bull moose to swing his five foot rack; to observe the feeding grizzly; or to just sit high on a mountain and drink in the grandeur, these are unforgettable pictures to hang in the parlor of memory. But there is something greater and more wonderful.

He made mountains so high you scarce see
    the sky—
Waters that roll like the thunder:
Heavens so blue till there's nothing so true,
How it moves the soul to wonder.

He made eagles to rest on crags dizzy crest,
Rivers in valleys of spender:
Hillsides on fire and the eyes never tire—

Just look and admire with wonder.

He made salmon to go where great rivers flow:
Horizons to make your mind wander:
God's garden of flowers in summer's soft
  shower—
You never get over the wonder.

He made snow glistening white through winter's
  long night;
Gold, and earth's treasure to plunder;
Aurora of stars through long arctic hours:
And men stand speechless with wonder.

It's a wonderful God who's done all of this;
Filled the great land with His splendor;
High mountains to sea that man's eye might
  see—
And all of it speaks of His wonder!

Capping it all in this wonder is the miracle of man and the
love of God for us. Some of us are beautiful people and
some are not so beautiful—yes, even ugly! We come in all
sizes, shapes, looks, and dispositions. The infinity of endless
space demonstrates the infinity of its Creator. "The heavens
declare the glory of God," and human beings declare it too
by their infinite variety.

Consider: seven billion of us, each with a patch of skin six
or eight inches by five inches wide we call our face, and
rarely two alike. And each one can be identified by a finger-
print or DNA code. Inner character is still different, often
unjudged by outer appearance.

The great colonial preacher, Jonathan Edwards, had a
pretty daughter he considered disagreeable. When her
boyfriend asked the preacher if he could marry her, Edwards

responded, "You can't have her."

"Why not," he asked. "She loves me and I love her!"

"Because she is not worthy of you."

The young man pressed, "But she is a Christian isn't she?"

"Yes," responded the preacher, "but the grace of God can live with some people no one else could ever live with."

Others of a more admirable spirit get along well with everybody. The very variety of God's creation speaks of His greatness and goodness.

One preacher was heard to say, "I would love the ministry if it wasn't for the people!"

Perhaps he would do better as a long haul truck driver. The heart of God is bigger than the universe he made with room for any and all.

"Come," says He, "Unto me all ye that labor and are heavy laden and I will give you rest."

The best of us needs the love of God provided in Jesus Christ. The worst of us can not get beyond it.

> How thou canst think so well of me and be the
>   God thou art,
> Is darkness to my intellect—but sunshine to my
>   heart.

Every true follower of the Savior King is "Looking for and hastening unto the coming of the Day of God" (2Peter 3:12). Nothing in this world will be just right until He comes, "Whose right it is."[1] The day is coming on fast when "every eye shall see Him."[2]

It is common nowadays to see people on some kind of crusade or another to save this world. Well meaning environmentalists have their costly agenda. The earth-centered mind is sure that science will ultimately fix everything, and so on. Not withstanding all the efforts of mankind, this world will never experience the real cure until the sin problem is completely cured, and the Son of God "whose right it is" is the only Physician who can do that. He is our hope, our only hope.

When He comes back on stage, it will be terrific to see what He will do for an encore. His first trip to earth was pretty incredible, considering the birth via the virgin, and following a torturous death, coming alive by His own power out of a sealed grave where He was laid certified dead! To say nothing of the awesome miracles He performed. Healing a dying boy six miles away, feeding several thousand with a boy's lunch, controlling violent storms, walking on water, giving eyesight to a man born blind, raising to life a four-day dead and buried man. A life impressively convincing to any but the hard hearted and closed minded.

Ah, but the description of events connected to His Second Coming are beyond anything we could dream or imagine. He is the Alpha and Omega—The beginning and the end. He is the subject, verb, and object of the last sentence. Bottom line: all in all.

Events are soon to take place in this world that will bring about unimagined changes to every one of us, and finally every knee shall bow in recognition that Jesus Christ is Lord. When all commerce is finished, all constructions turned on end, all the educating is over, the politics and economics, vocations, vacations, and recreations are blown to the wind, the single, remaining, all-important question is and will be "What is my relationship to the King of Kings, the Son of God?"

The common answers to the preacher's probing question about one's relationship to God and hope of Heaven are, "I'm OK," or "I'm doing my best," and "I attend church," and "I do good things to help people." All subheads under one heading: good works.

Human pride makes us think that good deeds, charity,

occasional sacrifice, and clean living are surely of more practical value than to simply accept the work and substitution of Christ Jesus on my behalf. Cain thought that way when he brought the fruit of his own labor to be accepted by God. Does it not prove my earnest desire to please God if I do something of a practical nature for Him? And will He not accept my gift and put it down in His record book to my account?

It's an idea that completely overlooks the awesome holiness of God, as contrasted with the total devastation sin has worked in this world of ours, and in our own hearts.

Isaiah says, "We are all as an unclean thing, and all our righteousnesses are as filthy rags" (Isaiah 64:1).

Cain's brother Able was accepted by God, not because he brought his own efforts, but because he submitted himself to God and followed the principle of faith and justification through the sacrifice of a sinless substitute (Hebrews 11:4).

If our own efforts to live rightly and do good could be offered to the holy God for acceptance, then it would have been absurd for God to give His own Son as a substitutionary sacrifice for us. He did so because there was and is no other way that salvation for our eternal souls could be secured except by the death, burial, and resurrection of Jesus Christ. King of Kings and Lord of Glory!

The Lord is There

Ezekiel 48:35

The ancient seer wrote The Words
of a distant golden age
When God the Mighty Maker comes
as promised to the sage.

The Hope and sunshine of this world
in a future to unfold
When Jesus comes to set things right
and the plans of God are told.

But, let God's finger write again
on the tablets of your heart
And know that He's not far away
in promises apart.

Far beyond my soul's best dreams
my Great God fills all things,
And all along this present road
He's now the King of Kings!

I will not fear a time to come
Tomorrow or next year,
When God forsakes His universe—
Or child that He holds dear!

I look behind and see His blood
Has washed my sins away.
I look ahead and there He stands
Still shepherding my way.

I look below and learn to trust

His everlasting arm
That holds me up and keeps me safe
From jeopardy and harm.

I look above, He's always there
To shelter from life's storm.
And best of all, He lives within
His purpose to perform!

Footnotes

Chapter 1
  1. John Newton, "Amazing Grace"

Chapter 3
  1. Mrs. H. S. Lehman, "What you Are"

Chapter 7
  1. II Corinthians 6:14–7:1

Chapter 11
  1. Author Unknown

Chapter 12
  1. Therron Babcock, "There's Been a Change in Me"

Chapter 16
  1. Elsie, Jack, and Jim in "Where the Roses Never Fade"

Chapter 17
  1. Ezekiel 21:27
  2. Revelation 1:7

Printed in the United States
3898

9 781931 232975